MW01119500

**New Directions for
Student Services**

Elizabeth J. Whitt
EDITOR-IN-CHIEF

John H. Schuh
ASSOCIATE EDITOR

Fostering the Increased Integration of Students with Disabilities

Marianne S. Huger

EDITOR

Number 134 • Summer 2011
Jossey-Bass
San Francisco

FOSTERING THE INCREASED INTEGRATION OF STUDENTS WITH DISABILITIES
Marianne S. Huger (ed.)
New Directions for Student Services, no. 134
Elizabeth J. Whitt, Editor-in-Chief
John H. Schuh, Associate Editor

NEW DIRECTIONS FOR STUDENT SERVICES (ISSN 0164-7970, e-ISSN 1536-0695) is part of The Jossey-Bass Higher and Adult Education Series and is published quarterly by Wiley Subscription Services, Inc., A Wiley Company, at Jossey-Bass, 989 Market Street, San Francisco, California 94103-1741. Periodicals Postage Paid at San Francisco, California, and at additional mailing offices. POSTMASTER: Send address changes to New Directions for Student Services, Jossey-Bass, 989 Market Street, San Francisco, CA 94103-1741.

New Directions for Student Services is indexed in CIJE: Current Index to Journals in Education (ERIC), Contents Pages in Education (T&F), Current Abstracts (EBSCO), Education Index/Abstracts (H.W. Wilson), Educational Research Abstracts Online (T&F), ERIC Database (Education Resources Information Center), and Higher Education Abstracts (Claremont Graduate University).

Microfilm copies of issues and articles are available in 16mm and 35mm, as well as microfiche in 105mm, through University Microfilms Inc., 300 North Zeeb Road, Ann Arbor, Michigan 48106-1346.

SUBSCRIPTIONS cost $89.00 for individuals and $259.00 for institutions, agencies, and libraries in the United States.

EDITORIAL CORRESPONDENCE should be sent to the Editor-in-Chief, Elizabeth J. Whitt, N473 Lindquist Center, The University of Iowa, Iowa City, IA 52242.

www.josseybass.com

Contents

EDITOR'S NOTES

As students with disabilities continue to pursue higher education in greater numbers, the need for comprehensive service provision has become a priority at many institutions in the United States. Students with disabilities were last addressed in a New Directions volume in 2000 and a lot has changed since then. Legal mandates and legislation, new paradigms for viewing disability services, and the diffusion of technology necessitate an updated guide.

This volume addresses higher education administrators and college professors beyond those working in the area of disabilities. All members of a community benefit from the diversity that students with disabilities bring to a campus, and all campus constituents have an obligation to serve their diverse students. Therefore, all members must be prepared to navigate issues surrounding the increased integration of students with disabilities with knowledge and professional preparation. This volume provides that preparation and knowledge. Disability services staff cannot be the only members of a college's administration who provide services to students with disabilities. If the campus is to take full advantage of the range of perspectives and talents that its students possess, increased integration is necessary.

This volume frames access to higher education within a contextual goal of increasing the social and academic integration of students with disabilities. To this end, all chapters provide practitioners and faculty members with guidance concerning not just accommodating but including students in the fabric of an institution.

In Chapter One, Marianne Huger discusses the value to all members of a campus community of a disability-friendly institutional climate. She offers practical suggestions for various constituencies to foster this environment. Next, John Salmen introduces the concepts of universal design and provides guidance to campuses that use these principles. Robert Shaw explores in Chapter Three how the concepts of universal design can be applied to learning and instruction. He includes specific examples of the benefit of these practices to students, faculty, and staff. In Chapter Four, Donna Korbel, Joan McGuire, Manju Banerjee, and Sue Saunders turn to the transition through college for students with disabilities and provide recommendations for services in this area. Elizabeth Case and Roseanna Davidson introduce in Chapter Five the accessibility of online learning and its advantages and challenges for students with disabilities. In Chapter Six, Heidi Soneson and Shelly Fisher speak to the importance of including students with disabilities in education-abroad opportunities. Holley Belch addresses in Chapter Seven the specific population of students with psychiatric disabilities and offers strategies for inclusion and integration in and

NEW DIRECTIONS FOR STUDENT SERVICES, no. 134, Summer 2011 © Wiley Periodicals, Inc.
Published online in Wiley Online Library (wileyonlinelibrary.com) • DOI: 10.1002/ss.389

outside the classroom. Jo Anne Simon closes the volume in Chapter Eight with an updated analysis of the legal issues that bear on higher education's inclusion and accommodation of students with disabilities.

This volume thus provides a foundational understanding of the importance of the full inclusion of students with disabilities in higher education. The exploration of universal design provides a further foundation into an underlying theory that may aid in increasing the academic and social integration of all students. The chapter authors also provide specific guidance on four issues that are currently paramount in serving students with disabilities: transition, online learning, Education-Abroad, and psychiatric disabilities. The volume ends with an exploration of the legal framework for fostering the increased integration of students with disabilities.

The chapter authors hope that readers gain insight and understanding pertaining to working with students with disabilities. Thinking about this population using many different lenses will aid in service provision and inclusion. It is our aim that this volume will provide these lenses.

Marianne S. Huger
Editor

MARIANNE S. HUGER is the assistant dean of students at American University and an adjunct instructor at the George Washington University, both in Washington, D.C. She was formerly the Director of Disability Services at Georgetown University Law Center.

NEW DIRECTIONS FOR STUDENT SERVICES • DOI: 10.1002/ss

1

All members of a campus community have a role to play in increasing the academic and social integration of students with disabilities.

Fostering a Disability-Friendly Institutional Climate

Marianne S. Huger

Students with disabilities are entering college at increasingly high rates due to legal mandates, sophisticated assistive technology, and improved access to educational accommodations. The 1990s saw an increase in offices of disability services on campuses throughout the United States. These offices evaluate documentation that students provide, approve appropriate accommodations, and ensure that accommodations are properly administered. The range of services and programs available to students with disabilities varies by institution (Getzel and McManus, 2005). All offices, however, are asked to provide increasingly varied and individualized services. In addition to the business of accommodation provision, offices of disability services are increasingly called on to find creative solutions in a difficult economy, provide guidance to offices on campus in order to improve accessibility, and advocate for students with disabilities. As institutions work toward a disability-friendly climate, the work of offices of disability services needs to be reenvisioned.

It no longer makes sense for these services to be the sole responsibility of one office or department. As Jones (1996) advises, disability work should be the responsibility of all units on campus rather than those whose sole responsibility is to oversee disability services. A campuswide commitment to increased accessibility and usability requires rethinking the mission of offices of disability services and building new partnerships with campus constituencies. Improving accessibility and inclusiveness is the job of the university as a whole. Offices of disability services can provide road maps for institutions as they commit to a culture shift to facilitate the full participation of all students, including those with disabilities.

NEW DIRECTIONS FOR STUDENT SERVICES, no. 134, Summer 2011 © Wiley Periodicals, Inc.
Published online in Wiley Online Library (wileyonlinelibrary.com) • DOI: 10.1002/ss.390

This culture shift will allow institutions to respond flexibly to the ever-changing needs of its student body. Rather than reacting to the accommodation requirements of individual students, a truly inclusive environment is prepared for and welcoming to a diverse population. As the campus climate opens, the need for individual accommodations will diminish.

This chapter discusses the value of the increased integration of students with disabilities on campus to the students with disabilities and those without disabilities. It then establishes that faculty, disability services practitioners, other administrators, and student leaders can play a vital role in increasing integration by providing practical guidance for each constituency.

A Disability-Friendly Climate: The Value to Students with Disabilities

Colleges and universities are decentralized by nature. In some instances, departments can operate seemingly independently, with little opportunity for collaboration. There is a great range in how offices of disability services interact with other departments on campus. Depending on the structure and mission of these offices, support services can be centralized or decentralized. This terminology refers to the amount of ownership and responsibility of issues related to disability (for example, student services, architectural considerations, and hiring practices) housed in a central office of disability services (Duffy and Gugerty, 2005). The chosen structure of disability offices can have great effects on the students that it serves.

The organization of institutions of higher education by department (such as the registrar, campus life, or academic departments) allows efficiency and specialization. However, it also requires students to navigate unfamiliar structures and cross invisible boundary lines in order to access the opportunities on campus that are most suitable to their interests and needs. This process can be detrimental to student learning and growth. A study by Dutta, Kundu, and Schiro-Geist (2009) found that students stated that the inadequate coordination of services for students with disabilities adversely affected their perception of the quality of these services. Students are recognizing the need for synchronization of services, and institutions must to find ways to meet this need.

Students do not think of themselves as consumers of distinct departmental resources and supports. They see themselves more holistically, and rightly so. For example, a student might be interested in international affairs. As administrators, we quickly parcel this conceptualization out into departmental silos: courses in international service, education abroad opportunities, and participation in internationally focused clubs and organizations. Absent an integration of services, students must work with a multitude of offices to create a coordinated college experience.

NEW DIRECTIONS FOR STUDENT SERVICES • DOI: 10.1002/ss

In order to facilitate appropriate accommodations, students with disabilities are required to identify departments and programs that they may need to access. A traditional model presumably requires a disability services practitioner to meet with a student individually to determine the accommodations necessary for each course and activity. The administrator then coordinates these accommodations with faculty, facilitates communication with the study-abroad office, and works with specific leaders of clubs and organizations to ensure the accessibility of its activities and meetings. In addition, the student would likely have additional requirements placed on him or her, such as communicating accommodation needs to faculty, detailing specifics of the disability to provide understanding by departmental administrators, and creatively problem-solving in order to facilitate access. This prepackaged approach works well for students who do not deviate from the preselected plan. This student, however, is rare.

Instead, students with disabilities change their minds and majors often, like any other student. They see themselves in the same holistic manner as other students do. The student referred to sees himself or herself as someone interested in international affairs, not as a bulleted list of courses and activities. By focusing on the accommodation needs of individual students, the institution puts a different burden on students with disabilities than it puts on others. These students must preplan their interactions to a degree that minimizes opportunities for spontaneous interaction and exploration. In addition, the need to self-identify and request services for participation in certain programs can lead students to think that they do not belong in the institution (Getzel and McManus, 2005).

An inclusive campus environment allows all students to interface with the community in a seamless and real-time manner. The philosophy of universal design, discussed in detail in Chapters Two and Three of this volume, provides promising guidance for creating such an environment. Students may attend university events, discuss course content with a professor during office hours, or eat dinner with friends without prior planning or coordination. If the environment is constructed in a way that assumes accessibility and inclusiveness, students with disabilities are more easily integrated into the academic and social fabric of an institution.

A college or university that views all students as members of the campus community who should be able to access all of its programs and services will realize a need for a new way to provide disability services. Disability services then become the job of each member of the community rather than of a handful of trained professionals. This student-focused mind-set must be pervasive throughout the institution in order for true inclusiveness to occur and needs to be supported at all levels of the institution.

An inclusive environment has clear benefits to students with disabilities. In an open campus, they are able to navigate bureaucracies easily, enjoy the benefits of being more academically and socially integrated, and explore the opportunities available at the institution. The benefits to the entire community are also significant.

A Disability-Friendly Climate: The Value to All Students

As student affairs professionals, we are concerned with the development and growth of students while they are in college (Evans, Forney, and Guido-DiBrito, 1998). One of the central tenets of student development theory is the idea that students grow by experiencing life events and then by making meaning of these events. Interacting with a diverse group of peers has the ability to enhance the learning environment of all students, furthering their growth and development. Thus, a diverse student body challenges the assumptions that students hold, allowing them "to examine and overcome preconceived ideas and stereotypes and to learn about people who are different from themselves within a context focused on openness, respect and learning" (McClellan and Larimore, 2009, p. 234).

A disability-friendly institutional climate increases all students' exposure to and interaction with peers with disabilities. Increased sensitivity to issues of difference is a valuable learning objective in college. Theories that underlie our conceptualization of prejudice can be translated to understand the role that the college can play in reducing students' discriminatory thoughts and actions, specifically toward people with disabilities. The minority group paradigm can be used to explain that membership in a minority group—in this case, people with disabilities—can imply commonalities among all members of the group (Jones, 1996). This theory acknowledges the role that environmental factors play in discrimination, prejudice, and marginalization.

Mere exposure theory, extended contact theory, and intergroup contact theory, along with the practical implications that these theories lend to student affairs professionals, can be employed to lessen these environmental factors by increasing the sensitivity of all students around issues of disability:

- *Mere exposure theory* is based on the idea that people have negative feeling about different groups if they are not exposed to these groups (Levy and Hughes, 2009). This theory holds that exposure can be gained from pictures or stories rather than from actual interaction. Prejudice is diminished, according to this theory, through increased exposure to diverse groups. If college administrators aim to minimize the prejudice students feel, mere exposure theory holds that simply exposing students to brochures or classroom examples that include people with disabilities would meet this end.
- *Extended contact theory* holds that an individual's prejudice against another group is diminished by knowing that others in the

individual's own group are associated with the other group (Levy and Hughes, 2009). Thus, a college student without a disability would be positively affected by being friends with someone who was friends with an individual with a disability. It follows that the ripple effects of integrating students with disabilities in the academic and social fabric of an institution could be great. According to extended contact theory, one friendship between a student without a disability and a student with a disability could modify the thinking patterns of a multitude of other students without disabilities.

• *Intergroup contact theory* states that individuals need actual contact with those different from themselves to reap the benefits of reduced prejudice (Levy and Hughes, 2009). According to this theory, mere exposure or tangential relationships with others are not enough. Students need to actually have personal and positive contact with members of other groups. Here, the academic and social integration of students with disabilities becomes vital. Friendships formed in residence halls, study groups, and student organizations are theorized to reduce prejudice.

As the workforce becomes more diverse, students graduating from college need to be comfortable working with those who are different from them, including those with disabilities. Mere exposure theory, extended contact theory, and intergroup contact theory all point to the same conclusion: greater academic and social integration of students with disabilities on campus holds benefits for all students. Faculty, disability services practitioners, other administrators, and student leaders must commit themselves to augmenting the level of integration on campus, given its potential for positive effects for students with disabilities and the student body as a whole.

Campus Constituency Involvement

An inclusive campus environment requires the support and assistance of all members of the community. As colleges and universities move from an accommodation model to an inclusion model, possibly through universal design practices, a greater number of individuals must understand their role in furthering the integration of students with disabilities.

All members of the campus community can facilitate and foster a more open learning and living environment. Faculty, disability services practitioners, other administrators, and student leaders are well positioned to pioneer these efforts. Small acts and adjustments can lead to big changes on a campus. The full inclusion of students with disabilities into the social and academic arenas of an institution is the job of the whole community.

Faculty. Faculty members are vital partners in accommodation provision and in increasing the inclusiveness of the educational environment. Faculty have been shown to be fairly open to providing needed

NEW DIRECTIONS FOR STUDENT SERVICES • DOI: 10.1002/ss

accommodations and academic adjustments (Houck, Asselin, Troutman, and Arrington, 1992; Nelson, Dodd, and Smith, 1990; Vasek, 2005), especially when they understand the connection between these actions and student success (Bourke, Strehorn, and Silver, 2000). Dutta, Kundu, and Schiro-Geist (2009), however, have cited an unfortunate lack of communication between staff in the office of disability services and faculty. This partnership is necessary for students to be fully integrated into academic life at the institution. Disability services practitioners can provide faculty with an understanding of disability services and accommodations if faculty are open to the conversation.

In addition to accommodation provision, faculty set the tone for the classroom climate. By using inclusive educational practices, faculty help to foster the academic integration of students with disabilities. Faculty are encouraged to:

- Evaluate students using multiple means (such as participation, written assignments, and exams) in order to allow students with various learning styles to demonstrate mastery of material
- Use course readings that are accessible or can be made accessible to students with disabilities
- Include people with disabilities in readings, classroom examples, and as guest speakers whenever possible
- Provide opportunities for work in groups that maximize the interactions of students, thereby increasing the comfort level of all students in cooperating with others of various levels of ability
- Become knowledgeable about the accommodation needs of students with various disabilities so as to be prepared to fully integrate all students in the educational experience
- Become familiar with the appropriate terminology to use when speaking about disability
- Use faculty governance structures to contribute to the inclusivity of the curriculum as a whole
- Maintain office space that allows all students to access office hours or outside assistance with course material

Disability Services Practitioners. Disability services practitioners are primarily responsible for providing appropriate educational accommodations. These specialists should work toward ensuring that the process for being granted and receiving accommodations is not overly burdensome. In addition to accommodation provision, offices of disability services can play a key role in increasing the integration of their target population with the general student body. These practitioners can provide a road map for their institution as it works to foster a more disability-friendly climate. Duffy and Gugerty (2005) advocate that "it is the role of disability services personnel to seek, nurture, and preserve institutional commitment and support for ensuring that students with disabilities have equal access to educational opportunities available to all other students" (pp. 89–90). To fulfill the expectation and mission disability services practitioners can:

- Maintain an up-to-date working knowledge of key legislation and case history so as to provide guidance on complying with federal and state law
- Provide training to faculty and staff regarding appropriate terminology, best practices for managing accommodations in the classroom, and suggestions for increasing access to offices and services
- Partner with technology services to ensure that platforms such as Web sites, course management tools, and e-mail systems are accessible to all students
- Work with students to identify impediments to integration and share these sentiments with campus constituencies so as to eliminate or minimize barriers

Other Administrators. Administrators other than those housed in offices of disability services can be key collaborators toward the goal of creating an inclusive environment for students with disabilities. Above all, administrators must be cognizant of the ways in which students interact with their offices and then determine how this interaction may be affected by various disabilities. A knowledgeable and sensitive administration is well positioned to foster integration. In this vein, all administrators should:

- Allow students to use programs and services through a variety of means (such as Web sites or in person) when possible
- Provide a departmental environment and physical space that allows all students to access personnel and resources
- Evaluate the accessibility of sponsored programs and services and work to minimize barriers for the integration of students with disabilities
- Collaborate with offices of disability services in order to understand the student population and appropriate terminology
- Visually represent people with disabilities in publications
- Practice nondiscriminatory hiring practices

Student Leaders. Student leaders often have considerable opportunities for interaction with administrators on campus and therefore are well equipped to learn about the diverse needs of students with disabilities. A heightened comfort level with those who are different from themselves will serve students well as they enter the workforce and continue to interact with people with disabilities.

Students are key to providing an open environment for all students to be integrated into the social fabric of an institution. In order to facilitate this social integration, student leaders should be encouraged to:

- Hold events and meetings exclusively at accessible venues, including on- and off-campus locations
- Bring speakers to campus who can address disability awareness
- Encourage the participation in clubs and activities of all students, regardless of level of ability
- Promote dialogue among students on subjects related to inclusion, stereotyping, and prejudice
- Find ways to increase students' level of comfort with students who are different from themselves by increasing inclusion and integration
- Explore means to foster the social integration of students with disabilities, remembering that social integration can be more difficult for students with disabilities than academic integration is

Conclusion

The increase of students with disabilities on college campuses requires institutions to reenvision how to serve this population. The partnership and collaboration of institutional departments will offer students with disabilities increased opportunities for academic and social integration. This increased integration has ripple effects that will contribute to the learning and growth of all students. The job of fostering a disability-friendly institutional climate cannot be done solely by an office of disability services. Practitioners in this office, as well as administrators in other offices, faculty, and student leaders, all play vital roles in opening a campus environment.

References

Bourke, A. B., Strehorn, K. C., and Silver, P. "Faculty Members' Provision of Instructional Accommodations to Students with LD." *Journal of Learning Disabilities*, 2000, *33*(1), 26–32.

Duffy, J. T., and Gugerty, J. "The Role of Disability Support Services." In E. E. Getzel and P. Wehman (eds.), *Going to College: Expanding Opportunities for People with Disabilities*. Baltimore, Md.: Brookes Publishing, 2005.

Dutta, A., Kundu, M. M., and Schiro-Geist, C. "Coordination of Postsecondary Transition Services for Students with Disabilities." *Journal of Rehabilitation*, 2009, *75*(1), 10–17.

Evans, N. J., Forney, D. S., and Guido-DiBrito, F. *Student Development in College: Theory, Research, and Practice*. San Francisco: Jossey-Bass, 1998.

Getzel, E. E., and McManus, S. "Expanding Support Services on Campus." In E. E. Getzel and P. Wehman (eds.), *Going to College: Expanding Opportunities for People with Disabilities*. Baltimore, Md.: Brookes Publishing, 2005.

Houck, C. K., Asselin, S. B., Troutman, G. C., and Arrington, J. M. "Students with Learning Disabilities in the University Environment: A Study of Faculty and Student Perceptions." *Journal of Learning Disabilities*, 1992, *25*(10), 678–684.

Jones, S. R. "Toward Inclusive Theory: Disability as Social Construction." *NASPA Journal*, 1996, *33*(4), 347–354.

Levy, S. R., and Hughes, J. M. "Development of Racial and Ethnic Prejudice among Children." In T. D. Nelson (ed.), *Handbook of Prejudice, Stereotyping, and Discrimination*. New York: Psychology Press, 2009.

McClellan, G. S., and Larimore, J. "The Changing Student Population." In G. S. McClellan and J. Stringer (eds.), *The Handbook of Student Affairs Administration*. (3rd ed.) San Francisco: Jossey-Bass, 2009.

Nelson, J. R., Dodd, J. M., and Smith, D. J. "Faculty Willingness to Accommodate Students with Learning Disabilities: A Comparison Among Academic Divisions." *Journal of Learning Disabilities*, 1990, *23*(3), 185–189.

Vasek, D. "Assessing the Knowledge Base of Faculty at a Private, Four-Year Institution. *College Student Journal*, 2005, *39*(2), 307–315.

MARIANNE S. HUGER is the assistant dean of students at American University and an adjunct instructor at the George Washington University, both in Washington, D.C. She was formerly the Director of Disability Services at Georgetown University Law Center.

2

Universal design has the potential to transform universities into truly egalitarian institutions that accommodate all users regardless of their size, age, or physical capabilities, allowing them to flourish, learn, and unleash their true potential.

Universal Design for Academic Facilities

John P. S. Salmen

Universal design (UD) is an evolving and expanding concept with varied definitions and meanings. Ultimately it is design that both allows access to a facility or element and facilitates users' empowerment. It is a concept that started in architecture, but is now being applied to an increasing number of fields of human endeavor, including the design of the Web, product design, housing for aging people. and academic curricula, to name but a few.

Universal design can play a role in many aspects of academic life and is often thought of in the context of learning. However, this chapter focuses on the impact of UD on the design of facilities in a university or campus setting. Universal design has the potential for transforming universities into truly egalitarian institutions that accommodate all users regardless of their size, age, or physical capabilities, allowing them to flourish, learn, and unleash their true potential. Universities are especially good facilities for the application of UD because they accommodate a wide range of transient users. Since one size does not necessarily fit all, the application of UD needs to be appropriate to the institution's scale, facility type, and program for it to be completely effective. Universal design accommodates not only people who use wheelchairs or are blind, but also older learners, parents with children, and nontraditional learners of all sorts. The effort to provide UD can also help institutions comply with the Americans with Disabilities Act (ADA), section 504 of the Rehabilitation Act of 1973, and other state and local accessibility regulations. This chapter explains the differences between accessibility and UD and discusses methods of accommodation and areas of opportunity for UD on campuses.

New Directions for Student Services, no. 134, Summer 2011 © Wiley Periodicals, Inc.
Published online in Wiley Online Library (wileyonlinelibrary.com) • DOI: 10.1002/ss.391

Accessibility Compliance Versus Universal Design

People frequently think that accessibility compliance and universal design are synonymous. They are not, and in fact, the difference between UD and accessibility is profound. Accessibility is about compliance with regulations that protect a small percentage of the population. Universal design is about empowering the entire population to reach its potential. Accessible design is accomplished through compliance with state, local, and national building codes and standards that establish a minimum level of design necessary to accommodate people with disabilities. Universal design is the art and practice of design to accommodate the widest variety and number of people throughout their life spans. It can be thought of as the process of embedding choice for all people into the things we create. As we learn about human needs and abilities and as new technologies develop, the practice of UD evolves and improves. In truth, it might be better to think of this field as universal designing, so as to focus on the decision-making process rather than some end product that may be improved in the future.

In the United States, three formal levels of guidance affect the accessibility of the built environment: laws, regulations, and standards. Laws are promulgated by a legislative body, such as the U.S. Congress or a state legislature, to address a public concern. An applicable law that guides accessibility is the ADA, which the U.S. Congress passed in 1990 to address discrimination against people with disabilities. Regulations are usually created by an enforcement agency of a government entity to implement a law. Standards are technical criteria defining compliance for an issue area.

The ADA is federal civil rights law. As such it is broad reaching and must be applied to situations even when no technical criteria are provided. The civil rights nature of the ADA and the resemblance of its criteria to building codes lead many to believe that compliance with only the technical criteria will ensure compliance with the law. This is not the case. When lawsuits that claim non-compliance with the non-discrimination requirements are embodied in the accessibility standards for facilities found in the ADA Title III, the courts are often turning to the spirit rather than the letter of the law. For instance, in movie theaters and sports arenas, seating for people with disabilities is supposed to provide lines of sight to the screen or playing field that is comparable to the lines of sight that other attendees have. Because there are no technical criteria for what *comparable* means, courts are making their own interpretations.

Universities must comply with a variety of federal laws and regulations, depending on the financing of the operations or facilities of each particular campus:

- The ADA covers all higher education facilities and requires access to programs, facilities, and services that are provided and open to the public. For state or local government institutions, Title II of the

ADA may also apply. The primary concept in the Title II regulations is program accessibility: the program when viewed in its entirety must be accessible, though not every element needs to be accessible. For example, if dormitories are provided for some students, some of the dormitories must be accessible, though all dormitory rooms are not required to provide accessibility features. The ADA Standards for Accessible Design set out the criteria that must be met in the design of new or renovation of existing campus facilities. (These standards were updated in 2010 and are now called the 2010 Standards.)

- If the university offers housing units with four or more units per building, the Fair Housing Act of 1988 applies. All ground-floor units and all units in buildings with elevators are considered "covered units" and must comply with accessibility guidelines.
- Section 504 of the Rehabilitation Act of 1973 requires that the programs of any recipient of federal funding, whether for research, construction, or programs, must be accessible when viewed in their entirety. This earlier law is similar to the ADA's Title II requirements, which apply to any institution receiving state or local funding. In addition, state laws, regulations, and standards often require compliance with a state building code. Most states have adopted the International Building Code and use its reference standard ICC/ANSI A117.1 for accessible and usable buildings and facilities.

It is vitally important for universities and colleges to follow federal, state, and local laws and regulations with their referenced standards, but embracing UD may be the best way to ensure compliance while also improving usability for the entire academic community. Universal design, however, is different from accessibility in that it does not have a set of standards. (The Global Universal Design Commission is currently developing voluntary UD standards for use in public buildings. See http://www.global universaldesign.org.) Voluntary efforts are the name of the game in UD, and they go beyond accessibility in many cases to provide usability for people regardless of their age or ability. Universal design is the process of embedding choice into the things we create for all people. Giving people options in the way that they use the environment is critical as our population becomes more diverse. Universal design is ultimately a process that empowers people by giving them more control over their lives and choice in the things that they do or the way in which they do those things.

Building on a collaboration with Ron Mace and I, Ruth Lusher used the term *universal design* in 1988 for an article in *Construction Specifier* magazine. We wanted to come up with a positive slant on accessibility requirements and to acknowledge the potential for good design that could be achieved by people who embrace the idea of making the world fit people better rather than looking at it as a regulatory requirement. North

Carolina State University's Center for Universal Design convened a number of experts at the end of the twentieth century to come up with principles of universal design. Seven were identified:

1. Equitable use
2. Flexibility in use
3. Simple and intuitive
4. Perceptible information
5. Tolerance for error
6. Low physical effort
7. Size and space for approach and use

These principles are a tool for analyzing facilities, products, and programs and helping to identify opportunities for enhancing usability through careful design selection. The principles embody goals, strategies, and objectives and can be found at the Center for Universal Design's Web site (http://www .design.ncsu.edu/cud/index.htm).

In short, accessibility is about compliance, and universal design is about design that empowers people. They are similar in that both affect the user-environment interface, However, UD has the potential for being for everyone, as opposed to a specialty element that benefits only a small population.

Methods of Accommodation

The wide variety of user abilities, coupled with the wide variety of academic and other programs, services, and facility types, implies an almost infinite number of possibilities for customizing the environment to accommodate individuals. Infinite customization is currently unrealistic for any organization or technology, but one method of accommodation is illuminated by comparing a fixed menu to a buffet. One of the key techniques of ensuring usability for a wide range of people is to provide a wide range of offerings, similar to a buffet, where a diner can select vegetarian, gluten-free, or high-protein meals or just dessert. A universally designed campus allows people choices of how they enter buildings, residential accommodations, and options for sitting in classrooms together or separately regardless of their mobility. Contrast this with a fixed-menu restaurant that attempts to satisfy everyone with one set of menu items and compare it with an old-style tiered classroom with fixed writing surfaces. Movable chairs on a tiered surface accessed by ramps allow a wide variety of users to participate in classroom experiences regardless of their size or space needs if the appropriate furniture is in place.

The concept of one-size-fits-all is elusive though not impossible. For example, an air door provides an entrance through which anybody can move regardless of abilities or limitations; however, an air door is a large energy consumer and may not be appropriate in a green society except in extreme circumstances. Usually, however, multiple methods provide choice that can fit a wide range of users. Where information is given, redundant modes of information delivery allow people to retrieve the information in more than one sensed modality. For example, alarms and warnings should be both visual (to warn people who cannot hear) and audible (for people who cannot see), or the menu at a food outlet could be available on a printed list for people who cannot hear, or staff can explain the menu or read it to a person who is visually impaired.

Trying to provide access by using only one method frequently can be costly and unaccommodating to some populations. Instead five methods of accommodation can be used to match users to the environment. Drawing on all of these methods in combination helps designers arrive at highly effective solutions that reach a broad population and in a cost-effective manner. These methods are:

- *Architecture.* Architecture refers to modifying the building, grounds, and other facilities, including ramps and doors, providing grab bars, and so on. The method is a permanent solution that provides long-lasting effect.
- *Personal assistance.* At the other end of the spectrum is the concept of providing direct assistance, such as readers or note takers for students who have visual limitations or hearing impairments. This is direct personal assistance from human to human. It is highly effective and very sensitive to the actual need, but it is expensive, must be maintained, and has the potential for affecting other human relationships in a detrimental fashion because dependence can breed power struggles.
- *Procedures.* Similar to personal assistance but implemented at the organizational level are changes of procedures. Procedures can be modified to accommodate physical limitations, for example. New methods or new technologies, such as Web-based learning, can allow people with mobility limitations to attend a class in a nonaccessible location. Another example is to offer tests in a non-time-constrained manner for students who have difficulty writing.
- *Equipment.* Equipment can be used to improve the human-environment interface. A variety of consumer products can make life easier. Automatic can openers for people with one hand and crank adapters for double-hung windows are examples.
- *Medical intervention.* Technology has allowed us to replace human body parts, provide drugs, and use prosthetic devices such as glasses or splints. Although these interventions are typically within the realm of medical practitioners or the individual, the aids and devices may provide an accommodation that empowers the person to do something on his or her own rather than being dependent on others.

NEW DIRECTIONS FOR STUDENT SERVICES • DOI: 10.1002/ss

Universities that understand these concepts and use these techniques can go beyond compliance with the minimum criteria found in accessibility regulations and create universally designed campuses and communities that empower all people.

Areas of Opportunity: Tips and Design Ideas

This section provides a few examples of areas of campus design where application of UD concepts can benefit all members of the academic community.

Grounds: Creating Choice in the Exterior Environment. Kutztown University in Kutztown, Pennsylvania, was built on a hilly site. Over the years, sidewalks were constructed between buildings, with stairs and often steep ramps that were difficult or impossible to use by students, faculty, and visitors with limited mobility. Universal Designers & Consultants (UD&C) helped the university's architect identify the accessible pedestrian paths and devise a system of directional signage and alternative accessible paths around barriers so that all students and visitors could navigate the campus. It promoted access in the most direct manner possible within an existing hilly environment.

A complaint against the university's accessibility had triggered a self-evaluation and the realization that pedestrian circulation could be improved for all students by identifying certain key paths within the campus that needed accessibility and allowing secondary paths to include nonaccessible-level changes where necessary to meet topographical conditions. This system provided at least one accessible route to every building, and in most cases multiple routes, allowing access to all programs using accessible routes.

An important part of this project was the need to provide information about where the accessible routes are located. This was done through maps provided on the university Web site, signage on the grounds, and pamphlets that are available to visitors indicating accessible entrances to buildings and accessible routes on the campus.

Classrooms and Assembly. Georgetown University Law School in Washington, D.C., wanted to respond to the needs of and requests from students with disabilities in a proactive rather than reactionary basis. UD&C staff worked with the disability services and facilities management departments to conduct a workshop with students to identify UD opportunities in a collaborative format. Participants identified a number of cost-effective ways to improve accessibility—for example:

- Modifying tables in classrooms to offer accessible seating
- Providing yardsticks for the bookstore manager to ensure merchandise aisles are wide enough for wheelchairs
- Recommending vertical-facing, instead of typical horizontal-facing, merchandise in the cafeteria refrigerated units

NEW DIRECTIONS FOR STUDENT SERVICES • DOI: 10.1002/ss

- Installing sensor-activated automatic doors in student residences to assist students with disabilities

Innovative and cost-effective solutions resulted from facilitated collaboration between students and the administration, and in the process, providing an excellent model for use at other universities.

The Student Athletic Building at the George Washington University in Washington, D.C., built in the 1960s, presented many barriers to students with disabilities as participants in or spectators at student athletic events. When the university decided to refurbish the building, one of the highest priorities was to provide access to all areas for students who are unable to climb stairs. To ensure this, the university required the selected design firm to hire a third-party accessibility and UD expert, and UD&C was engaged.

The building was originally equipped with two small elevators that created great congestion at the time of sporting events. Adding an elevator and reworking exterior access relieved congestion and provided accessible paths to all areas. In addition, spectator and other common use areas were enhanced to accommodate not only people who have physical limitations but also people who want privacy for cultural reasons. Among the additions were:

- Dispersed accessible seating
- Audio and visual scoreboards
- Multiheight counters at food vending areas
- Tables and seating areas with accessible knee and toe clearance
- Family rest rooms for those who needed assistance
- Private and accessible public showers and lockers

These changes empowered the entire student body. Recreation is an important aspect of rehabilitation for many people, allowing them to maintain their self-image and their strength, especially after a traumatic injury.

Residential. Students and faculty with disabilities come in all sizes, shapes, and colors. Their residential needs therefore reflect the range found in the general public, such as individual students out of high school, married students with children, and adult learners who want communal residential environments. Accordingly, accessibility should be provided in all types of residences that are provided on campus, from dormitories to married student housing, and sorority and fraternity housing to conference housing.

Roll-in showers in residence halls allow people who have mobility limitations to bathe safely and conveniently. Other people may choose to have soaking tubs to allow them to relax after a long day. Dormitory buildings laid out for wheelchair accessibility assist not only students in wheelchairs but also students with bicycles and everyone else, especially on moving day.

Conclusion

Academic planners who understand and use UD can incorporate choice into the design of university programs, services, and facilities. In this way, they will allow the broad range of students, faculty, and visitors to interact and create the types of academic communities that empower and liberate everyone through higher education.

Appendix: Additional Resources

Americans with Disabilities Act (ADA) Home Page: The US Department of Justice established this web site to provide information about, and technical assistance on, the Americans with Disabilities Act (ADA). (http://www.ada.gov)

   Association on Higher Education and Accessibility (AHEAD): A professional membership organization for individuals involved in the development of policy and in the provision of quality services to meet the needs of persons with disabilities involved in all areas of higher education. (http://www.ahead.org)

   Center for Inclusive Design and Environmental Access (IDEA Center), SUNY at Buffalo: dedicated to making environments and products more usable, safer, and healthier in response to the needs of an increasingly diverse population. (http://www.ap.buffalo.edu/idea/)

   UniversalDesign.com: A broad-based, philanthropic web site that supports the growth of the Universal Design industry through information, commerce, and professional networking. (http://www.UniversalDesign.com)

   Universal Designers & Consultants, Inc.: A team of expert architect and design professionals who provide Universal Design and Accessibility Consulting services to business owners and companies who want to improve customer access and make their establishments compliant with the Americans with Disabilities Act and/or the Fair Housing Act. (http://www.UDConsultants.com)

References

1 Americans with Disabilities Act of 1990, Pub. L. No. 101-336, § 2, 104 Stat. 328 (1991).
2 International Code Council, Inc. *American National Standard: Accessible and Usable Buildings and Facilities (ICC/ANSI A117.1-1998)*. Falls Church, VA: 1998.
3 Lusher, R. H., "Designing for the Life Span." *Construction Specifier,* February 1988, pp. 22–24.
4 Section 504 of the 1973 Rehabilitation Act, Pub. L. No. 93-112, 87 Stat. 394 (Sept. 26, 1973).

JOHN P. S. SALMEN is the president of Universal Designers and Consultants in Takoma Park, Maryland.

3

College courses can be designed without special
accommodations and be accessible for diverse students.

Employing Universal Design for Instruction

Robert A. Shaw

Students vary immensely in their prior knowledge of course material, learning style, reading speed, English language proficiency, inclination to speak with the instructor outside class, and other characteristics too numerous to list. Among the individual differences that have drawn the most attention in education are various forms of disability.

Schools and colleges have long struggled with ways to provide an educational environment appropriate for students with disabilities. Federal law requires that colleges and universities make "reasonable accommodations" for students with documented disabilities. Determining reasonable accommodations for this subset of students requires significant investments of time and money from the student and the institution. The process also requires students with disabilities to be proactive in requesting accommodations and requires hair-splitting decisions by administrative staff in determining which accommodations are required for each individual student. The accommodations process serves only some of the students with disabilities at an institution and does nothing to help meet the educational needs of other students.

Universal design for instruction (UDI) is an approach to course design that seeks to create an appropriate learning environment for all students, including those with disabilities. (Several similar terms are used to refer to the idea of applying principles of universal design to teaching: universal design for instruction, universal design for learning, and universal course design. The terms differ in emphasis, but all have in common the idea that instructional procedures should be designed to be accessible to the maximum

NEW DIRECTIONS FOR STUDENT SERVICES, no. 134, Summer 2011 © Wiley Periodicals, Inc.
Published online in Wiley Online Library (wileyonlinelibrary.com) • DOI: 10.1002/ss.392

number of people.) This approach also helps other students to learn the course material in ways most appropriate to their individual learning needs. When done well, this approach has benefits for students with and without documented disabilities, faculty, and staff at the institution. This chapter discusses the flexible curricular practices and technology that constitute UDI and provides specific examples of how these practices have benefited students in a number of institutions of higher education. The appendix lists four organizations that provide a wealth of materials and examples to help colleges that are beginning to implement a UDI strategy.

Components of Universal Design for Instruction

Universal design for instruction evolved from the concept of universal design in architecture (see Chapter Two, this volume). This concept, developed by the Center for Universal Design (1997) at North Carolina State University, has seven principles:

1. Equitable use
2. Flexibility in use
3. Simple and intuitive
4. Perceptible information
5. Tolerance for error
6. Low physical effort
7. Size and space for approach and use

College faculty at a number of institutions have realized that these same basic principles would be beneficial in instruction. Different groups have applied these principles to the instructional process in different ways. For example, the Disabilities, Opportunities, Internetworking, and Technology (DO-IT) Center at the University of Washington has used these seven principles and developed extensive guidelines for how to apply the principles to college instruction (Burgstahler, 2009). Faculty at the Center on Postsecondary Education and Disability at the University of Connecticut adapted these principles by adding two more that are particularly relevant to the instructional process (McGuire and Scott, 2006):

> Principle 8: A community of learners. The instructional environment promotes interaction and communication among students and between students and faculty.

> Principle 9: Instructional climate. Instruction is designed to be welcoming and inclusive. High expectations are espoused for all students [p. 129].

Researchers at the Center for Applied Special Technology (CAST) in Massachusetts took a different approach, applying concepts from neuroscience to

NEW DIRECTIONS FOR STUDENT SERVICES • DOI: 10.1002/ss

the basic idea of universal design to develop three principles for universal design for learning (National Center on Universal Design for Learning, n.d.):

- Multiple means of representation, to give learners various ways of acquiring information and knowledge
- Multiple means of action and expression, to provide learners alternatives for demonstrating what they know
- Multiple means of engagement, to tap into learners' interests, offer appropriate challenges, and increase motivation

The researchers at CAST initially developed ways to use digital technology to implement these principles in K-12 classrooms, but the principles apply equally well to instruction at the college level.

The use of UDI in a course will not necessarily eliminate the need for individual accommodations for certain students. However, if a course is designed from the start or redesigned with attention to the different ways that students engage with information and express what they have learned, the need for individual accommodations will be greatly reduced or even eliminated, and the engagement and understanding of all students in the course will be strengthened.

The Need for UDI

The student population in colleges and universities in the United States is becoming increasingly diverse in terms of ethnicity, age, social class, country of origin, and disability status. Meeting the educational needs of this diverse population requires a new way of thinking about instructional access. Universal design for instruction moves the paradigm relating to instructional access from accommodation to full inclusion (McGuire and Scott, 2006).

Providing reasonable accommodations for students with documented disabilities does nothing to address the needs of other students with particular learning needs, and it does a poor job of meeting the needs of many students with disabilities. Those of us who have worked in disability support services know of many students who struggle with a traditional learning environment but have never considered getting a formal diagnosis or cannot afford the costly diagnostic procedures. Other students who have a documented diagnosis are reluctant to disclose this to the institution and do not request accommodations. Meanwhile, students for whom English is a second language, students with temporary disabilities, students with pressing family issues, and students with learning styles that do not match the structure of a particular course receive no support from policies designed to provide reasonable accommodations.

An accommodation model places the problem, whether due to a disability or a different ethnic, age, or socioeconomic background, with the

NEW DIRECTIONS FOR STUDENT SERVICES • DOI: 10.1002/ss

nontraditional student. That is, the lack of fit between the traditional instructional process and the student is seen as a deficit in the student. A UDI model instead seeks to create an instructional environment that is flexible enough to serve the needs of a wide variety of students. The examples in the next section show the variety of ways in which this can be accomplished.

Examples of UDI in College Classrooms

Some applications of UDI are high tech, involving electronic manifestations of the course materials, podcasting of lectures, and other digital resources. Many others are low tech, involving minor changes in the course procedures.

The Ivy Access initiative (2004) was a five-year project based at Brown University that provided support for faculty at Brown and four other institutions to incorporate principles of universal design into their courses. A series of workshops and ongoing faculty discussion groups introduced the principles of universal design to interested faculty and gathered information on the practices they found successful. The workshops followed this design model:

1. Determine the essential components of the course.
2. Provide clear expectations and feedback.
3. Incorporate natural supports for learning: clear statement of course objectives, opportunities to ask questions, frequent exercises to assess understanding.
4. Use multimodal instructional methods.
5. Provide a variety of ways of demonstrating knowledge.
6. Use technology to enhance learning.
7. Encourage faculty-student contact.
8. Start where you feel comfortable. Go one step at a time; add one or two UDI components to your course and see how they work. Then add another.

More specifically, participants in the workshops were asked to incorporate into their courses CAST's three universal design principles:

Multiple Means of Representation

- Generous use of graphic displays of the course concepts on projected images and whiteboard
- Simulations—electronic animations or skits by class members
- Models
- A clear and complete syllabus

- Assignments presented in written form and posted on a course Web site
- Accessible electronic materials for students with perceptual impairments
- Lecture outlines or notes distributed in class or posted on a course Web site (or both)
- Study guides
- Summary of major concepts
- Accessible Web content
- Accessible multimedia

Multiple Means of Engagement

- Small group discussions, whole class discussions, lectures, fishbowl debates, and so on
- A variety of homework assignments—for example, readings, exercises, group projects, tutorials, and Web searches
- Teaching of explicit strategies to learn the material

Multiple Means of Expression

- A variety of graded exercises (papers, exams, homework, presentations)
- Multiple formats on examinations (essay, short answer, oral, and so on)
- Choices on graded exercises (for example, a choice of a final exam, a final paper, or a class presentation or Web site)
- Sufficient time on examinations for all students
- Allowed use of word processing, spell check, and grammar check on in-class exercises

Faculty members at the five institutions made a number of changes in their courses during the Ivy Access project—for example:

- A sociology professor revised her syllabus to specify the objectives more clearly and added three short papers in addition to the midterm and final exam. This change helps students structure the material in the course and provides more diversity in the types of work that affect the final course grade.
- A math faculty member posted overhead visuals on his course Web site so that students could use them for reference and review. He also began to deliver his lectures more carefully, replacing general terms like *this* or *that* with more specific descriptions, pausing to emphasize key points, and making eye contact with his students to assess their understanding of the lecture.

- A composition faculty member began taping his class and making the tapes available to students so they could review class discussion and instructions about assignments.
- A foreign language professor developed puppet shows, role plays, Velcro cards, and searches of computer Web sites in the second language to make the instruction as multimodal as possible.
- An education professor allowed students the choice of writing the final exam as a take-home or a three-hour in-class final. He was not sure which option would be the more popular one. It turned out that almost exactly half the students chose each option each semester. Despite his initial concerns about the equivalence of the two forms of the final exam, he found that he was able to grade the two types of exams equitably.
- Two universities provided student assistants to help faculty make their course Web pages and in-class media fully accessible.
- A geology professor developed computer animation modules to illustrate some of the key concepts in a course on physical hydrology. These are shown in class and are available online as well.
- After students complained that they had no context to understand the lectures in a computer science course, the professor started each class with a forecast of the key concepts to be discussed that day and why they were important to the course material.
- An introductory physics course administered midterm exams in the evening, outside the normal class schedule, allowing all students up to two and a half hours for what was traditionally a one-hour exam. Some students used the additional time to complete the exam; others reported that simply knowing the additional time was available took some of the stress out of the exam even if they did not use the additional time.
- A biology professor introduced new topics by asking all students to write a short essay on a topic in class. Some students are better writers than talkers, and the professor found that this practice led to more widespread participation in the subsequent class discussions.
- A biology professor began using two projectors in his lectures so he could leave each slide on the screen longer. He also posted the graphics on the course Web site so students could preview them before class and review them after class.
- Professors in a number of disciplines found that online chat rooms or asynchronous bulletin boards allowed students who are shy about speaking in class to participate actively in on-line discussions.

Faculty members at a number of other institutions have provided examples and guidelines about how to incorporate principles of universal design into courses:

NEW DIRECTIONS FOR STUDENT SERVICES • DOI: 10.1002/ss

- The Equity and Excellence in Higher Education project at the University of Massachusetts Boston has developed a ten-minute online tutorial about how to design a syllabus that incorporates principles of universal design (http://media.umb.edu/syllabustutorial/). These syllabi decrease confusion about course logistics, are easy to read, and provide information in both printed and digital form, which gives students a choice in how to access the information (Equity and Excellence in Higher Education, n.d.).
- Ruth J. Fink, long-time director of disability services at the University of Colorado at Boulder, posted a classic essay on the disability service providers' listserv (DSSHE-L) discussing how professors who rely on pop quizzes might accomplish the same ends with practices that do not unduly disrupt the flow of the class and also do not penalize students with slow processing times (including students with learning disabilities, English as second language, or even those who are sleep deprived). Among her suggestions were posting the questions on the course Web site and having students e-mail or post the answers there, using small group or whole class discussions to assess students' understanding of the material, and including the questions on the course syllabus, to be turned in on specified days. She concluded with the imminently sensible suggestion that professors consult with the disability services office, other faculty members, and students to analyze the purposes of the pop quizzes and how to accomplish the same ends in other ways (Fink, 2001).
- The UDI Online Project Team at the University of Connecticut developed guidelines for UDI in online and blended courses (2009). Among their suggestions are:
  - Fostering maximum attention to learning by being aware of screen structure and layout of Web site features (breaking down a construct into multiple pages with headings)
  - Taking advantage of electronic communications technology by fostering communication among students in and out of class by structuring study groups, discussion groups, project groups, and chat rooms
  - Making a personal connection with students through video or phone
- David Rose and his colleagues at CAST developed a course on UDL at the Harvard Graduate School of Education (Rose, Harbour, and Johnston, 2006). Their description of the course design provides a fine example of how to apply principles of universal design to course lectures, discussion groups, and textbooks. The course lectures are videotaped and posted on the Web for all students to review or catch up on a missed lecture.

On a rotating schedule, a few students each week are required to post their notes from the lecture on the course Web site. The variety of note-taking styles is a strong example of the diverse ways in which different students approach the same lecture, and the notes generate a robust discussion on the course Web site. The course has two kinds of optional discussion groups—one that focuses on a review of the week's lecture and the other on an advanced discussion of the concepts. Each group is conducted both online and face-to-face. Students can choose to attend neither, either, or both types of discussions, in whichever modality fits their schedule and preferred mode of interaction. Students have a choice of two textbooks for the course—one that is more text based and one that is more graphics based. Throughout the course, students are given multiple options for accessing the course information and participating in the course activities.

- Stephen Rehberg, at the Georgia Institute of Technology, and Peggy Brickman, at the University of Georgia, experimented with ways to make a large lecture course accessible for students with disabilities as well as all other students. In a large biology course, they ensured that the electronic documents were fully accessible and created electronic discussion threads in the learning management system. They also broke the class up into groups of six to seven students who engaged in collaborative note-taking exercises to reinforce the course material. Students in the course reported that the responsibilities associated with this exercise forced them to be better organized and focus more on the lectures. Students with disabilities who might otherwise have requested the accommodation of a professional note taker had access to the notes of a number of fellow students, and all students benefited from the careful attention to their notes that their peers provided (Kolowich, 2010).

These examples illustrate the wide variety of practices that increase the accessibility of courses for students with disabilities and diverse backgrounds and learning styles. None alters the content of the course or substantially alters the basic structure of the course. Many of the faculty who participated in the Ivy Access workshops at Brown and the other universities in the project reported that the UDI process deepened their understanding of their course objectives and ways of assessing whether those objectives have been met.

Benefits of UDI

The process of planning and carrying out universal design principles in a curriculum provides benefits for all constituents of the institution: students, faculty, and administrative staff.

NEW DIRECTIONS FOR STUDENT SERVICES • DOI: 10.1002/ss

Students with disabilities have increased access to course participation with fewer special accommodations. In most cases, they can participate fully in courses without needing to be treated as a different class of student and without needing to take the time and psychic energy to arrange individual accommodations. Universal design for instruction also increases access to course participation for students with temporary illnesses, different learning styles, varied backgrounds in the subject matter, limited English proficiency, and other factors that can affect course participation. A flexible course format allows all students to approach the course and demonstrate their understanding of the course material in the way most appropriate for them and their individual circumstances.

Universal design for instruction benefits faculty in a number of ways. First, the process of examining the essential components of a course and thinking about how to convey these in the most accessible way is a useful exercise for any faculty member. The UDI process provides a context for rigorous thinking about pedagogy. Second, UDI reduces the number of students who need individual accommodations, saving the faculty member considerable time. It is not unusual for a professor to have four or five students with documented disabilities in a given course, with each needing somewhat different individual accommodations. Providing these individual accommodations can take considerable time for each exercise—time that can be better spent in other ways if the course structure provides the flexibility the students need for the exercises. Finally, UDI can improve the accuracy of the assessments of all students in a course. Done well, UDI eliminates many of the barriers to accurate assessment for students with many individual differences. Universal design for instruction allows assessments to reflect the students' knowledge of course material rather than extraneous factors.

Disability support service professionals spend a great deal of their time arranging and implementing individual accommodations for students: meeting with students to determine eligibility for accommodations, notifying professors of the need for individual accommodations, and overseeing accommodations such as separate examination facilities and note-taking services.

As faculty implement principles of UDI in their courses, disability service professionals are able to spend time instead in collaborative partnerships with faculty and other staff members on course design and advocacy activities.

Professional Development for UDI

Institutions that have been successful in implementing UDI have created support structures to help faculty with this process. Three of the centers that have been developing professional development models for UDI are the DO-IT program at the University of Washington (Burgstahler and Cory,

2008), the Center on Postsecondary Education and Diversity at the University of Connecticut (Scott and McGuire, 2008), and the Equity and Excellence (E&E) in Higher Education project at the University of Massachusetts-Boston (Behling and Hart, 2008). These three centers are presented as particularly visible examples; many other institutions are also carrying out effective professional development in UDI.

Researchers at the E&E project identify three realities that faculty must acknowledge when they are trying to implement new approaches to pedagogy:

- College faculty often claim lack of resources and time to make changes in their pedagogy.
- The easier a concept is to understand and implement, the more likely faculty will adopt it.
- Faculty are more willing to apply principles of universal design if they can recognize how the principles will affect students from culturally, socioeconomically, and academically diverse backgrounds.

To address these realities, the E&E project recommends the use of three tools:

- An easily accessible Web site to provide information and examples for faculty (its Web site is www.eeonline.org)
- A peer support team to assist faculty who are implementing universal design in their courses, consisting of representatives of offices such as disability support services, information technology, cultural diversity, the library, and the center for teaching excellence
- Examples from a variety of disciplines to provide models of possible changes in pedagogy

The E&E project invites a small group of faculty to meet regularly with the core team throughout a semester to learn the principles of universal design and implement these in their courses. These faculty members then become mentors for colleagues in future semesters (Behling and Hart, 2008).

The Center on Postsecondary Education and Disability at the University of Connecticut is one of the pioneers in implementing UDI in postsecondary institutions. Its current project, UDI Online, provides support for faculty members who are developing online and blended instruction courses to help them incorporate UDI principles into these courses (http://www.udi.uconn.edu/). Center staff provide a set of electronic tools that can be applied to online and technology blended courses as well as online instruction in the principles of UDI and a wide range of examples.

The DO-IT project at the University of Washington has developed a checklist to guide faculty who are incorporating universal design into their courses (Burgstahler, 2010). The checklist incorporates suggestions from a wide variety of universal design projects around the country and has been used by forty-eight postsecondary institutions to help faculty implement principles of universal design in their teaching.

The Role of College Administrators

College administrators play a key role in facilitating the use of universal design in the curriculum and other aspects of the college environment. Providing professional development and support services for faculty to implement universal design in their courses is one important way to do this. Including disability issues in all campus policies and practices is another essential step. Chapter Two in this volume discussed the need for universal design of the physical facilities of the institution. Other aspects of the campus can also have universal design features:

- Policies and announcements regarding student services should be available in accessible formats.
- Campus publications should have clear information available to students and faculty about the process for requesting reasonable accommodations that might be needed even in a UDI course.
- The staff in all campus life offices (counseling center, health services center, career services, and so on) should be trained to be aware of issues that might confront student with disabilities.
- The institution's education abroad program should have explicit published policies for students with disabilities (see Chapter Six, this volume).
- The institution's course evaluation process should address issues of disability, as should campus hiring procedures. Creating a committee to monitor campus accessibility, both physical and nonphysical, will help to ensure that all aspects of the campus are accessible for the maximum number of students.

One of the most effective things that a college administration can do is to appoint a single person to be responsible for campus accessibility issues, including universal design. It is important that students, faculty, and staff know whom to ask about accessibility issues, and it is equally important to have someone who is charged with initiating and overseeing universal design activities.

Good Teaching Is Good Teaching

In 1987, Harriet Sheridan, then dean of the College at Brown University, produced a videotape entitled *Effective Teaching for Dyslexic/All College Students.* Interviews with students with learning disabilities at Brown University and

Dartmouth College illustrated teaching procedures that are helpful to all students: a respectful environment, material presented clearly and through more than one modality, frequent and immediate feedback, and opportunities for active learning. The same year, Arthur Chickering and Zelda Gamson published their influential list of *Seven Principles for Good Practice in Undergraduate Education* (Chickering and Gamson, 1987). Those principles continue to be an excellent guide for teaching any student, and the practices described in this chapter are extensions of these principles inspired by attention to the needs of students with disabilities but beneficial for all students.

Appendix: Resources

The following organizations have been particularly active in promulgating universal design for instruction in postsecondary education. Anyone considering a UDI initiative can begin by consulting their materials:

- Center for Applied Special Technology: http://www.cast.org/
- University of Massachusetts—Boston Equity & Excellence in Higher Education: http://www.eeonline.org
- University of Connecticut UDI Online: http://www.udi.uconn.edu/
- University of Washington Disability Opportunities Internetworking and Technology Center: http://www.washington.edu/doit/

References

Behling, K., and Hart, D. "Universal Course Design: A Model for Professional Development." In S. E. Burgstahler and R. C. Cory (eds.), *Universal Design in Higher Education: From Principles to Practice.* Cambridge, Mass.: Harvard Education Press, 2008.

Burgstahler, S. "Universal Design of Instruction (UDI): Definition, Principles, Guidelines, and Examples." 2009. https://www.washington.edu/doit/Brochures/PDF/instruction.pdf.

Burgstahler, S. "A Checklist for Inclusive Teaching." 2010. Retrieved Mar. 10, 2010, from http://www.washington.edu/doit/Brochures/Academics/equal_access_udi.html.

Burgstahler, S. E., and Cory, R. C. "Indicators of Institutional Change." In S. E. Burgstahler and R. C. Cory (eds.), *Universal Design in Higher Education: From Principles to Practice.* Cambridge, Mass.: Harvard Education Press, 2008.

Center for Universal Design. "The Principles of Universal Design." 1997. Retrieved Sept. 14, 2010, from http://www.ncsu.edu/www/ncsu/design/sod5/cud/about_ud/udprinciplestext.htm.

Chickering, A. W., and Gamson, Z. F. *Seven Principles for Good Practice in Undergraduate Education.* Washington, D.C.: American Association for Higher Education, 1987. (ED 282 491)

Equity and Excellence in Higher Education. "Universally Designing a Syllabus." N.d. Retrieved Mar. 27, 2010, from http://media.umb.edu/syllabustutorial/.

Fink, R. J. "The Accommodation Dilemma of Pop Quizzes." 2001. Retrieved Mar. 27, 2010, from http://dss.cua.edu/Providing%20Equal%20Access%20in%20the%20Classroom/popquizes.cfm.

Ivy Access Initiative. "Implementing Universal Instructional Design in College Courses." 2004. Retrieved Mar. 10, 2010, from http://www.brown.edu/Administration /Sheridan_Center/docs/uid.pdf.

Kolowich, S. "For One, for All." *Inside Higher Ed*, July 19, 2010. Retrieved July 19, 2010, from http://www.insidehighered.com/news/2010/07/19/notetaking.

McGuire, J. M., and Scott, S. S. "Universal Design for Instruction: Extending the Universal Design Paradigm to College Instruction." *Journal of Postsecondary Education and Disability*, 2006, *19*(2), 124–134.

National Center on Universal Design for Learning. "UDL Guidelines, Version 1.0." N.d. Retrieved July 17, 2010, from http://www.udlcenter.org/aboutudl/udlguidelines.

Rose, D. H., Harbour, W. S., and Johnston, C. S. "Universal Design for Learning in Postsecondary Education: Reflections on Principles and Their Application." *Journal of Postsecondary Education and Disability*, 2006, *19*(2), 135–151.

Scott, S. S., and McGuire, J. M. "A Case Study Approach to Promote Practical Application of Universal Design for Instruction." In S. E. Burgstahler and R. C. Cory (eds.), *Universal Design in Higher Education: From Principles to Practice*. Cambridge, Mass.: Harvard Education Press, 2008.

Sheridan, H. W., producer. *Effective Teaching for Dyslexic/All College Students*. Providence, R.I.: Sheridan Center for Teaching and Learning, Brown University, 1987. Video.

UDI Online Project Team. "Examples of UDI in Online and Blended Courses." Storrs, Conn.: UDI Online Project, University of Connecticut, 2009. Retrieved Apr. 10, 2010, from http://www.udi.uconn.edu.

ROBERT A. SHAW is dean of the School of Education at Westminster College in Salt Lake City, Utah.

NEW DIRECTIONS FOR STUDENT SERVICES • DOI: 10.1002/ss

4

*Student affairs professionals have an opportunity to
promote active student engagement and improve the
experiences of students with disabilities by embracing a
collaborative and inclusive model of practice.*

Transition Strategies to Ensure Active Student Engagement

*Donna M. Korbel, Joan M. McGuire, Manju Banerjee,
Sue A. Saunders*

Transition into college for students with disabilities has been written about extensively over the past decade, due in part to legislative mandates implemented at the secondary level. With significant increases in the number of these students in the college population, a focus on their transition through college is imperative to improve retention and graduation outcomes that have a compelling relationship to subsequent wage-earning power (U.S. Census Bureau, 2002). Student affairs professionals across units have an opportunity to promote active student engagement and improve the experiences of students with disabilities by embracing a collaborative and inclusive model of practice based on self-determination and principles of universal design. This chapter identifies demographic trends, issues, and challenges that characterize the postsecondary landscape; presents a collaborative model of college transition services; and offers recommendations at each stage of the transition services continuum.

The constructs of self-determination and universal design offer guidance and a theoretical framework for practitioners committed to engaging students with disabilities in their transitions during college. According to Gerber (2009), issues of empowerment and self-determination are at the heart of successful transition for these students, whether it is into postsecondary education or employment. Self-determination encompasses an array of skills, knowledge, and beliefs that facilitate an individual's engagement in goal-directed, self-regulated behavior (Field and others, 1998). A critical component of self-determination is the ability to self-advocate, that is, to engage in

New Directions for Student Services, no. 134, Summer 2011 © Wiley Periodicals, Inc.
Published online in Wiley Online Library (wileyonlinelibrary.com) • DOI: 10.1002/ss.393

personal goal setting and exercise decision making (Kochhar-Bryant, 2003). The numerous choices facing college students across social, academic, and personal domains offer opportunities for student affairs personnel to reinforce decision making and personal growth that build on personal responsibility and self-awareness. Given compelling research on the connection between students' self-determination skills, academic success, and post – high school outcomes (Goldberg, Higgins, Raskind, and Herman, 2003; Konrad and others, 2007), a service delivery philosophy based on the values of self-determination and self-advocacy should permeate student affairs.

Another concept to enhance student engagement and practices is universal design (see Chapters Two and Three, this volume). Historically, disabilities have been viewed as defects or deficiencies in individuals that set them apart from most other people, leading to a response of fixing or remedying what is perceived as wrong or providing assistance that can be viewed as special consideration of those who are disabled (Wolanin and Steele, 2004) rather than a more inclusive approach. This medical model is giving way to a social model of disability that espouses the belief that disability is a natural part of the human condition and shifts the focus to disabling environments or social circumstances. Related to this model is universal design, a concept from the field of architecture described as "the design of products and environments to be usable by all people, to the greatest extent possible without the need for adaptation or specialized design" (Center for Universal Design, 1997). Common examples are building ramps, automated sliding doors, and curb cuts. When architects put the concept of universal design into practice, they are guided by seven design principles (Center for Universal Design, 1997):

- Equitable use
- Flexibility in use
- Simple and intuitive
- Perceptible information
- Tolerance for error
- Low physical effort
- Size and space for approach and use

Extending the concept of universal design to the instructional environment (Scott, McGuire, and Foley, 2003) and student affairs holds the promise of making a campus welcoming, accessible, and usable for everyone (Burgstahler, 2008). The idea is to anticipate diversity (for example, gender, age, race, ethnicity, culture, learning styles, native language) and intentionally design instruction and services for students with a broad range of characteristics. More practical suggestions for inclusive student services based on self-determination and universal design follow.

Although collaborative partnerships are frequently discussed in the student affairs literature, little has been written about how to structure and use such arrangements to foster successful transitions for students with disabilities. Several factors warrant consideration when adopting a systemic approach that can promote active student engagement. Changing demographics among college populations, as well as issues and challenges that are unique for students with disabilities, are important catalysts for designing a cohesive and responsive approach across student affairs units.

The Changing Postsecondary Landscape

President Barack Obama has articulated his administration's higher education policy and noted that "education is the economic issue of our time" (Kim, 2010). He has suggested that by 2020, the United States should increase the number of college graduates by 8 million, noting that the country has fallen from number 1 to number 12 in college graduation rates for young adults in a single generation. Enrollments are rapidly increasing, with over 19 million students currently in U.S. colleges and universities, representing an annual growth rate of 4 percent (Knapp, Kelly-Reid, and Ginder, 2010). Concurrently this is a period of dwindling resources; unstable funding sources; ever changing technology; larger class sizes; increased emphasis on evaluation, assessment, outcomes, and accountability; changing student demographics; and the need for extensive student support systems (Grund, 2010; Jacobs and Hyman, 2009; Rothstein, 2008; Shaw, 2009).

Students with disabilities comprise a sector of this changing population. According to the National Center for Education Statistics (Knapp, Kelly-Reid, and Ginder, 2010), nearly 11 percent of enrolled students report having a disability. The National Council on Disability estimates that the percentage is closer to 17 percent (Kessler Foundation and the National Organization on Disability, 2010). In addition to increased numbers of students with disabilities, the complexities of the types of disabilities have changed dramatically and now include students with psychiatric disorders, chronic health conditions, autism spectrum disorders, and severe food and environmental allergies (Harbour, 2009; U.S. Government Accountability Office, 2009). U.S. armed forces veterans of the post-9/11 era are another growing student population with disabilities such as traumatic brain injury, posttraumatic stress disorder, late-acquired blindness or deafness, significantly disfiguring burns, and multiple amputations (Church, 2009). Resources available to them through the Post-9/11 Veterans Educational Assistance Act of 2008 ensure that colleges can expect increasing numbers of these students. Students with intellectual disabilities (also defined as mental retardation) are now seeking access to higher education, with particular attention directed to them in the Higher Education Opportunity Act of 2008. These students will have very different goals and needs and may benefit more from life skills and employment training than from services traditionally provided by colleges and universities.

New Directions for Student Services • DOI: 10.1002/ss

Another factor that affects the transition of students with disabilities to college is legislation. Regulations pertaining to postsecondary students with disabilities are vastly different from those for the K-12 system (McGuire, 2010), and the implications for student affairs personnel can be challenging. Under the Americans with Disabilities Act, a civil rights statute, and its amendments (2008), qualified students with disabilities must have equal access to all programs and services at the postsecondary level. In the K-12 system, these students are entitled to a free, appropriate, public education by the Individuals with Disabilities Education Improvement Act of 2004. Based on this law, many traditional-age students with disabilities have had individualized instruction, advocacy services, and extensive accommodations during their previous schooling experience. Students whose parents have assumed a strident advocacy role, sometimes disparagingly described as "helicopter" parents (Kochhar-Bryant, 2010), have adopted a passive coping style instead of engaging in self-advocacy. As a result, these students' ability to take charge and engage in goal setting and decision making often is weak, which can create significant challenges for them in a college environment.

Finally, technology is a factor with major implications for college students with disabilities. Up until the late 1990s computer skills were the only technological competencies required of college students for a general baccalaureate degree. This view has undergone a radical transformation. Offerings of online and blended courses have steadily increased (Allen and Seaman, 2007; see also Chapter Five, this volume), and many institutions of higher education have technology-competency requirements for graduation (for example, University of Connecticut, 2010). Faculty are expanding their use of instructional or learning technologies in their teaching and communication with students using Web-based instructional delivery platforms such as Blackboard. It is now increasingly important for students with disabilities to be familiar not only with assistive technologies (for example, taped textbooks, FM systems to aid listening, "talking" calculators) but also with instructional technology, defined as hardware (computers, smartphones), software, and the Internet (Banerjee, 2010).

Technological preparedness has become a requirement for all college students, including those with disabilities. Yet research suggests that students with learning disabilities or attention deficit hyperactivity disorder are less comfortable than their nondisabled peers with learning technologies (Parker and Banerjee, 2007). As part of the transition planning process, college-bound students with disabilities should be prepared for the types of accommodations in college that may be technology based, such as text-to-speech software, rather than a reader. Awareness of the ways in which technology has transformed and continues to shape postsecondary education is an important element in delivering student services and promoting student engagement, and student affairs personnel can expect to work with students with disabilities who will use technology for academic, social, and personal tasks.

Keeping abreast of the impact of the factors that are changing the college environment is important as student affairs units move ahead in examining their identity and planning for change. The next section describes a collaborative model for student engagement that is relevant across student affairs units.

Implementing a Collaborative Approach

Collaboration among student affairs units, as well as strategic partnerships with entities outside student affairs and beyond the campus borders, are vigorously advocated, especially since fiscal realities mandate more efficient use of resources (American College Personnel Association and National Association of Student Personnel Administrators, 2010). A cooperative approach engenders benefits beyond simply improving service delivery or increasing student engagement. For instance, if disability services units partner with residential life and student activities to expand the involvement of students with disabilities in leadership development programs, that collaboration fosters the development of shared assumptions about the value of universal design that could lead to improved procedures and practices for all students, whether they are pursuing leadership activities or not (Keeling and others, 2004). Well-developed collaborations can create healthy cultural norms among participating units that can "transform working relationships and re-focus energy away from competition and the maintenance of silos toward cross-functional planning and shared responsibility" (Keeling and others, 2004, p. 69).

Redefining the Roles and Structures of Student Affairs

The transition services continuum outlines a systemwide approach to transition planning and therefore requires not only collaboration but also rethinking the responsibilities of student affairs professionals. Redesigned roles and structures require a specific delineation of responsibilities at the start of the collaboration process in order to avoid disagreement about who is responsible for what. Since cross-unit collaboration often requires sharing fiscal or staff resources, any reallocation of these must be explicitly spelled out. Furthermore, when sharing information across offices, it is critical to outline procedures that respect confidentiality and professional ethics while also making sure that all appropriate offices have the student information needed to provide comprehensive services. For example, a prerequisite to collaboration between counseling center personnel and disability services to assist a particular student is informed consent on the part of the student to share relevant information. This is an ideal example of the importance of self-determination that reinforces student engagement.

Given changing student demographics, a starting point for redefining roles and responsibilities may begin with disability services providers'

NEW DIRECTIONS FOR STUDENT SERVICES • DOI: 10.1002/ss

delivering accurate information to the campus community about character-istics of specific disabilities (for example, Asperger's syndrome or posttrau-matic stress disorder) annually or using Web-based resources. Student affairs colleagues could collaboratively brainstorm particular engagement strategies that are congruent with the culture of the institution and have a demonstrable positive outcome. A compendium of strategies could be col-lected and provided to all staff members to use as they work with students across stages of the transition continuum. Strategies that reflect universal design should be clear and straightforward, with consideration given to physical environments that may unintentionally restrict access because of distractions, space restrictions, or limitations in technology access.

The student affairs profession, regardless of functional area or institu-tional context, shares a common set of core values rooted in four funda-mental philosophical traditions: holism, humanism, pragmatism, and individualism (Winston and Saunders, 1991). These values complement the values of self-determination and universal design and offer a framework for implementing a collaborative approach. One practical suggestion is for student affairs division leaders to make these core values, as well as self-determination and universal design, an explicit part of orientation for new staff, staff retreats, communiqués, and marketing materials. These values can be made explicit through strategic planning documents or mission and vision statements. It is also essential that students with disabilities are clearly identified as an important subgroup of an institution's increasingly diverse student population.

Finally, redesigned roles and structures that effectively foster transi-tions of students with disabilities should avoid the narrow focus on col-laboration within student affairs units only. If effective transitions are to be an institutional priority, the perspectives of these students and those who serve them should be present at the president's table (Keeling and others, 2004). Depending on organizational structure and culture, the means to advocate for transition services will vary, but the importance of promoting collaborative transition strategies for students with disabilities remains an institution-wide priority.

Collaborative Transition Strategies

In order to create effective transitions for students, various units within the institution must collaborate in ways that foster meaningful communication and flexibility in meeting a wide variety of student issues and concerns. Tran-sitions begin well before matriculation and include strategies to assist stu-dents as they exit the collegiate environment. Therefore institutions must plan ahead for such transitions, creating partnerships across the university that are intentional about collaborating to design meaningful programs.

Preadmission Strategies. A partnership between the disability services unit and admissions offices, financial aid services, orientation, and public relations is essential to raise awareness about inclusion in the preadmission phase of transition. As noted in the transition services continuum, a significant portion of the process occurs before admission and even before application to a particular institution.

A welcoming and inclusive environment is communicated most powerfully through less obvious means, such as who is pictured on the institution's Web site or whether students with disabilities are included in statements outlining diverse subpopulations. Powerful indicators of an inclusive campus climate are the ability of all staff to easily and uniformly answer questions about how the institution works with students with disabilities and messages that communicate the positive contributions of students with disabilities to the campus environment (for example, feature stories in a campus newspaper or alumni publication). Given the current level of technology penetration into postsecondary education, preadmission efforts to raise student awareness of requirements for technology competencies necessary for college are essential. Information sessions for prospective students must include details about assistive as well as commonly used learning technologies such as course management systems (for example, Blackboard). Assistive technology is defined in federal legislation (Technology-Related Assistance for Individuals with Disabilities Act, 1988) as "any item, piece of equipment, or product system whether acquired commercially off the shelf, modified or customized, that is used to increase, maintain, or improve functional capabilities of individuals with disabilities." In-house availability or collaboration with personnel who have expertise and experience in both technologies is a necessity.

Strategies During Enrollment. Across the continuum, all support services can enhance student engagement by crafting internal policies and protocol that address accommodations, access, and service delivery. For example, to promote self-determination, campus personnel who provide academic advising could use an interview protocol that asks students to list their learning strengths and weaknesses and includes an optional disability disclosure statement. Advisors should be familiar with any institutional policy relating to students with disabilities, such as course substitutions and reduced course load. Education abroad programs should have accurate information about the accommodation process in international colleges and universities (see Chapter Six, this volume). Disability services offices can promote autonomy and self-determination so that students can be made increasingly responsible for their own access needs. To illustrate this, a self-help scanning station would allow students to independently create text in an alternate media format. Career services can anticipate questions from students with nonvisible disabilities about the wisdom of disclosing a disability during a job interview and be prepared with objective and factual guidance.

Since effective transitions involve cocurricular engagement, intentional collaboration between disability services providers and units that emphasize involvement (residential life, student activities, fraternity and sorority life, community service, and so on) is needed. Educating staff and student leaders about universal design and self-determination principles, as well as legal mandates, is an important first step in making the rich collection of activities welcoming to all students. Conversations with campus personnel who design and maintain Web sites, including those that provide up-to-date facts about student activities and options, are critical to ensure that students have the opportunity to locate institutional information (hyperlinks), ask questions, and receive announcements and updates. Accessibility features to ensure usability by students with disabilities are essential in underscoring the importance of universal design principles.

Reflected in the transition services continuum is the fact that some students with disabilities desire enhanced services beyond the fundamental access services that are legally mandated, for example, accommodations and auxiliary aids (U.S. Government Accountability Office, 2009). Fee-based services that are individualized and designed to promote student success are permissible (U.S. Government Accountability Office, 2009), yet their cost can be prohibitive. This reality requires that student affairs professionals develop new sources of funding through gifts, corporate sponsorship, and grants from government agencies or private foundations. Campus personnel with expertise in finding and obtaining external funding sources can be a valuable resource. In addition, some student affairs vice presidents are creating development or advancement units within their own divisions. Collaborating with these units can sometimes provide a revenue stream to offset the costs of enhanced services.

Shifts in enrollment patterns also have implications for the delivery of student affairs services along the transition services continuum. Nontraditional students are often unable to meet during traditional office hours, creating potential roadblocks to effective academic advising, counseling, and other time-bound supports. Extending the hours that a service office remains open or offering virtual office hours are options that exemplify an inclusive philosophy and reinforce student engagement. Considering recent statistics that 92 percent of college students log into Facebook and spend an average of 147 minutes there each week ("Shutdown Shot Down," 2010), thinking creatively is warranted in terms of tapping into alternative methods of communicating with students. Personnel in campus units such as academic advising centers, counseling offices, and mental health and disability services, as well as faculty, might consider connecting through commonly used social media such as Facebook and Twitter. Every student affairs unit should engage in a self-study to determine whether alternative methods of communication are available such that students with hearing or visual impairments have equal access.

Transition Exit Strategies. Just as preadmission planning is essential for effective transition into college, the move from college to employment or graduate studies also warrants planning. Internships provide excellent

NEW DIRECTIONS FOR STUDENT SERVICES • DOI: 10.1002/ss

opportunities for students to reflect on the match between specific jobs and their strengths, weaknesses, and preferences. Contact with career services and academic programs to explore and plan for such options should begin early, and many career offices offer information sessions for students initiating the search. If elements such as academic advising and career planning have been effectively used along the transition services continuum, students will be well prepared for such exit tasks as applying and taking required entrance exams for graduate and professional studies. Familiarity with the process for requesting accommodations on these exams is important because each testing agency has its own procedure and time lines for reviewing documentation to determine an applicant's qualifications for accommodations (Brinckerhoff and McGuire, 2010). Students should also be aware that there is no guarantee that accommodations used in college will be granted for standardized professional and graduate studies exams. Disability services professionals can work collaboratively with career services, as well as directly with students, to address questions of disability self-disclosure during job interviews and anticipated workplace accommodations.

Self-awareness is critical in the transition to employment. Students should be aware of workplace supports, including human resource person-nel who may be a preferred source of advice about self-disclosure. The question of workplace accommodations centers on the essential elements of a job and what comprises a reasonable accommodation. With planning that extends across the transition services continuum, students can be well positioned to enter the workforce with the skills and self-knowledge to be successful in their chosen career.

Discussion

A recent report by the U.S. Government Accountability Office (2009) underscores the importance of collaboration between disability services and other campus offices. The notion of an office for students with disabili-ties comprising a one-stop center that can address the needs of a diverse and growing population is no longer advisable and may not be in the best interest of students. Cooperation across campus functions such as counsel-ing services, financial aid, housing, academic departments, student activi-ties, study abroad, and career services is essential not only to ensure equal access to all programs and services, a legal mandate, but also to promote student development and preparation for employment. Such a collaborative model would also tap into areas of staff expertise, an important element given the array of supports that can benefit students. The transition ser-vices continuum provides a planning tool to initiate a collaborative and systemic approach to inclusive transition strategies.

Although student success is most typically associated with the impor-tant outcomes of retention and degree completion, focusing on only these outcome variables is questionable given the wide array of needs presented by students with disabilities as well as other diverse learners (American College Personnel Association and National Association of Student Personnel Administrators, 2010). If institutions are to make a meaningful impact on transitions for students with disabilities, they must attend to and assess such process dimensions as student engagement, the quality of the learning environment, and the availability of academic and social supports. The sage advice of the professional organizations for student affairs should be heeded: "Sixty years of research on college impact demonstrates that the most important factor in student success—more important than incoming student characteristics—is student engagement, that is, students' investment of time and effort in educationally purposeful activities" (American College Personnel Association and National Association of Student Personnel Administrators, 2010, p. 8).

References

"About UD." *The College of Design at North Carolina State University.* N.d. Retrieved Mar. 18, 2011, from http://www.adaptenv.org/index.php?option=Content&Itemid=26.

Allen, I. E., and Seaman, J. "Online Nation: Five Years of Growth in Online Learning." *The Sloan Consortium,* 2007. Retrieved Dec. 10, 2010, from http://sloanconsortium.org/publications/survey/online_nation.

American College Personnel Association and National Association of Student Personnel Administrators. *Envisioning the Future of Student Affairs.* Washington, D.C.: American College Personnel Association and National Association of Student Personnel Administrators, 2010.

Americans with Disabilities Act Amendment Act. U.S. Code. Title 4, §§ 12101 et seq. 2008.

Banerjee, M. "Technology Trends and Transition for Students with Disabilities." In S. F. Shaw, J. W. Madaus, and L. L. Dukes III (eds.), *Preparing Students with Disabilities for College: A Practical Guide for Transition.* Baltimore, Md.: Brookes Publishing, 2010.

Brinckerhoff, L. C., and McGuire, J. M. "Getting to Know Your Way Around High Stakes Testing Accommodations." Paper presented at 22nd Annual Postsecondary Disability Training Institute, Saratoga Springs, N.Y., June 2010.

Burgstahler, S. E. "Universal Design of Student Services: From Principles to Practice." In S. E. Burgstahler and Rebecca C. Cory (eds.), *Universal Design in Higher Education: From Principles to Practice.* Cambridge, Mass.: Harvard Education Press, 2008.

Center for Universal Design. "The Principles of Universal Design." *The College of Design at North Carolina State University,* 1997. Retrieved Mar. 18, 2011, from http://www.adaptenv.org/index.php?option=Content&Itemid=Center for Universal Design.

Church, T. E. "Returning Veterans on Campus with War Related Injuries and the Long Road Back Home." *Journal of Postsecondary Education and Disability,* 2009, 22(1), 43–52.

Field, S., and others. "Self-Determination for Persons with Disabilities: A Position Statement of the Division on Career Development and Transition." *Career Development for Exceptional Individuals,* 1998, 21, 113–128.

Gerber, P. J. "Transition and Adults with Learning Disabilities." In P. J. Gerber and others (eds.), *Learning to Achieve: A Review of the Research Literature on Serving Adults with Learning Disabilities.* Washington, D.C.: National Institute for Literacy, 2009.

Goldberg, R. J., Higgins, E. L., Raskind, M. H., and Herman, K. L. "Predictors of Success in Individuals with Learning Disabilities: A Qualitative Analysis of a Twenty-Year Longitudinal Study." *Learning Disabilities Research and Practice*, 2003, *18*, 222–236.

Grund, N. "Mapping the Future of Student Affairs: Task Force Highlights Opportunities and Challenges." *Leadership Exchange*, Summer 2010, pp. 10–15.

Harbour, W. S. "The Relationship Between Institutional Unit and Administrative Features of Disability Services Offices in Higher Education." *Journal of Postsecondary Education and Disability*, 2009, *21*(3), 138–154.

Higher Education Opportunity Act. U.S. Code. Title 20, §§ 1001 note. 2008.

Individuals with Disabilities Education Improvement Act. U.S. Code. Title 20, §§ 1400 et seq. 2004.

Jacobs, L. F., and Hyman, J. S. "Seventeen Ways College Campuses Are Changing." *U.S. News & World Report*, May 20, 2009. Retrieved Dec. 20, 2010, from http://www.careercollegecentral.com/news/17_ways_campuses_changing.

Keeling, R. P., and others. *Learning Reconsidered: A Campus-Wide Focus on the Student Experience*. Washington, D.C.: American College Personnel Association and National Association of Student Personnel Administrators, 2004.

Kessler Foundation and the National Organization on Disability, Harris Interactive. *2010 Survey of Americans with Disabilities*. New York: Kessler Foundation and the National Organization on Disability, Harris Interactive, 2010. Retrieved Dec. 20, 2010, from http://www.2010disabilitysurveys.org/.

Kim, J. "Highlights of President Obama's Speech on Higher Education Aug. 9, 2010." Web log comment. Retrieved Dec. 20, 2010, from http://www.insidehighered.com/blogs/technology_and_learning/highlights_of_president_obama_s_speech_on_higher_education.

Knapp, L. G., Kelly-Reid, J. E., and Ginder, S. A. *Postsecondary Institutions and Price of Attendance in the United States: Fall 2009, Degrees and Other Awards Conferred: 2008–09, and Twelve-Month Enrollment: 2008–09*. Washington, D.C.: National Center for Education Statistics, 2010. Retrieved Mar. 18, 2011, from http://nces.ed.gov/pubs2010/2010161.pdf

Kochhar-Bryant, C. A. "Introduction to Transition." In G. Greene and C. Kochhar-Bryant, *Pathways to Successful Transition for Youth with Disabilities*. Upper Saddle River, N.J.: Pearson Education, 2003.

Kochhar-Bryant, C. A. "How Secondary Personnel Can Work with Families to Foster Effective Transition Planning." In S. F. Shaw, J. W. Madaus, and L. L. Dukes (eds.), *Preparing Students with Disabilities for College: A Practical Guide for Transition*. Baltimore, Md.: Brookes Publishing, 2010.

Konrad, M., and others. "Self-Determination Interventions on the Academic Skills of Students with Learning Disabilities." *Learning Disability Quarterly*, 2007, *30*, 89–113.

McGuire, J. M. "Considerations for the Transition to College." In S. F. Shaw, J. W. Madaus, and L. L. Dukes (eds.), *Preparing Students with Disabilities for College: A Practical Guide for Transition*. Baltimore, Md.: Brookes Publishing, 2010.

Parker, D. R., and Banerjee, M. "Leveling the Digital Playing Field: Assessing the Learning Technology Needs of College-Bound Students with LD and/or ADHD." *Assessment for Effective Intervention*, 2007, *33*, 5–14.

Post 9-11 Veterans Educations Assistance Act of 2008. Public Law 252. 110th Cong., 2nd sess., June 30, 2008.

Rothstein, L. "Millennials and Disability Law: Revisiting Southeastern Community College v. Davis (September 10, 2008)." *Journal of College and University Law*, 2007, *34*(1). Retrieved Mar. 18, 2011, from http://ssrn.com/abstract=1266333.

Scott, S. S., McGuire, J. M., and Foley, T. E. "Universal Design for Instruction: A Framework for Anticipating and Responding to Disability and Other Diverse Learning Needs in the College Classroom." *Equity and Excellence in Education*, 2003, *36*, 40–49.

Shaw, S. F. "Transition to Postsecondary Education." *Focus on Exceptional Children,* 2009, 42(2), 1–16.

"Shutdown Shot Down." *Inside Higher Education,* Sept. 16, 2010. Retrieved Dec. 20, 2010, from http://www.insidehighered.com/news/2010/09/16/harrisburg2.

Technology-Related Assistance for Individuals with Disabilities Act. U.S. Code. Title 29, §§ 2201 et seq. 1988.

U.S. Census Bureau. *The Big Payoff: Educational Attainment and Synthetic Estimates of Work-Life Earnings.* Washington, D.C.: Government Printing Office, 2002. Retrieved Dec. 20, 2010, from http://www.census.gov/prod/2002pubs/p23-210.pdf.

U.S. Government Accountability Office. *Higher Education and Disability: Education Needs a Coordinated Approach to Improve Its Assistance to Schools in Supporting Students.* Washington, D.C.: Government Printing Office, Oct. 2009. Retrieved Dec. 20, 2010, from http://www.gao.gov/new.items/d1033.pdf.

University of Connecticut. *University of Connecticut General Education Guidelines.* 2010. Retrieved Dec. 20, 2010, from http://geoc.uconn.edu/geocguidelines.htm.

Winston, R. B., and Saunders, S. A. "Ethical Practice in Student Affairs." In T. K. Miller and R. B. Winston (eds.), *Administration and Leadership in Student Affairs: Actualizing Student Development in Higher Education.* (2nd ed.) Muncie, Ind.: Accelerated Development Press, 1991.

Wolanin, T. R., and Steele, P. E. *Higher Education Opportunities for Students with Disabilities: A Primer for Policymakers.* Washington, D.C.: Institute for Higher Education Policy, 2004.

DONNA M. KORBEL *is the Assistant Vice President of Student Affairs and also maintains her role as the Director of the Center for Students with Disabilities at the University of Connecticut in Storrs.*

JOAN M. MCGUIRE *is a professor emerita of special education and Senior Research Scholar at the University of Connecticut Center on Postsecondary Education and Disability in Storrs.*

MANJU BANERJEE *is associate director of the Center for Students with Disabilities and associate research scholar at the Center for Postsecondary Education and Disability, both at the University of Connecticut in Storrs.*

SUE A. SAUNDERS *is extension professor and coordinator of the Higher Education and Student Affairs Master's Program at the University of Connecticut in Storrs.*

5

*With the majority of public postsecondary institutions
offering online or hybrid credit courses and 11 percent of
postsecondary students having a documented disability,
the accessibility of online courses cannot be ignored.*

Accessible Online Learning

D. Elizabeth Case, Roseanna C. Davidson

The number of online courses offered at the postsecondary level is increasing at a rate greater than the increase in overall higher education enrollment, with approximately one of every four higher education students taking at least one course online (Allen and Seaman, 2009). In the 2006-07 academic year, 97 percent of public two-year and 88 percent of public four-year postsecondary institutions offered college-level online or hybrid credit courses (Parsad and Lewis, 2008). In 2008, students with disabilities represented nearly 11 percent of all postsecondary students (U.S. Government Accountability Office, 2009), yet whether students with disabilities can access these courses is rarely considered (Kinash, Crichton, and Kim-Rupnow, 2004). Rowland (2000) found that only 25 percent of college and university Web pages were accessible to individuals with disabilities (Rowland, 2000), and the accessibility of postsecondary Web sites continues to be a concern (Fichten, Ferraro, Asuncion, Chwojka, Barile, Nguyen, Klomp, and Wolforth, 2009; Parton, Hancock, and Oescher, 2009). Making technology such as online learning accessible is ethically appropriate, economically sensible, and self-serving, as everyone may need accessible technology as the population grows older. And it is also the law (Coombs, 2000).

A number of laws, standards, and guidelines exist to help make online courses accessible to students with disabilities. The 1990 Americans with Disabilities Act prohibits discrimination based on disability that would prevent participation in "the services, programs, or activities of a public entity." Section 504 of the Rehabilitation Act of 1973 similarly prohibits discrimination based on disability by any program or activity that receives federal funding, and section 508 provides specific guidelines on how to

NEW DIRECTIONS FOR STUDENT SERVICES, no. 134, Summer 2011 © Wiley Periodicals, Inc.
Published online in Wiley Online Library (wileyonlinelibrary.com) • DOI: 10.1002/ss.394

make Web sites accessible. The World Wide Web Consortium also provides detailed recommendations for accessible Web sites, although these guidelines do not carry the force of law. Accessibility of online courses is included as well in the Higher Education Opportunity Act (2008), which established an advisory commission on accessible instructional materials and allocated money for professional development and technical support on accessibility. (See Chapter Eight, this volume.)

Students with Disabilities in Online Courses

Students with disabilities cannot be denied the opportunity to take online courses, assuming they meet the academic prerequisites required of all students for the course. However, like all other students, those with disabilities should consider their own preferred learning style to determine if an online course provides a good fit. For example, online courses are best for students who are strong self-learners. Students who prefer to have information explained to them or who benefit from lively class discussions will probably not thrive in online courses. In addition, most of the steps required to create accessible materials are simple and do not require much additional time and effort.

Advantages. Online courses can be particularly beneficial to students with disabilities. The flexibility of working from home at any hour of the day helps students who have numerous doctor appointments or medications that affect their ability to focus at certain times of the day. Students with mobility or transportation difficulties, weakened immune systems, or other challenges that make attending a traditional face-to-face course difficult appreciate the ability to work from home.

Some students benefit from working on course work more frequently for shorter periods of time at each sitting. For example, instead of attending a class for seventy-five minutes twice a week, a student can log into the class several times during the week for just a twenty-minute session. In addition, students can review online course materials as often as needed instead of relying on a single lecture presentation.

Many online courses use bulletin boards for student interaction. Some students with disabilities are hesitant to participate in live class discussions because they need more time than most other students to collect and organize their thoughts or because they have impaired speech. Online discussions allow students the time needed to consider and edit their comments, and speech problems are not apparent in typed communication. Deaf students can communicate directly with their peers without the intervention of an interpreter.

Disadvantages. Online courses require self-discipline, good time management, and the ability to work independently. Some disabilities make this more difficult. In addition, a larger amount of reading is usually required in online courses than in face-to-face courses. Students with disabilities related to reading may have more difficulty in online courses as a result.

Note that we do not address accessibility as a disadvantage. Students should not avoid online courses, and teachers and advisors should not dissuade students from taking online courses because of the extra work to make them accessible. If course designers are proactive and make online courses accessible as they are created, then students need only consider personality and learning styles when deciding whether take an online course, not whether the course will be accessible to them.

Importance of Proactive Design

Most adjustments needed in order to make online courses accessible are fairly easy and inexpensive if accessibility is taken into consideration at the time the course is created. It is much more difficult, time-consuming, and expensive to retrofit a course to make it accessible after a student with a disability has enrolled in the course.

Making courses accessible at the time of creation also helps avoid a last-minute scramble to meet student needs. Properly adapting an inaccessible course may take more time than is available, resulting in a poorly designed site and stress for the faculty, Web designers, disability counselors, and the students involved.

Because making courses accessible as they are designed costs little in time, effort, and resources, there is no disadvantage in doing this work from the start. Accessible course design benefits all students, not just those with disabilities. However, most departments already have a number of courses that have been created without attention to accessibility, and a plan should be created for addressing their accessibility. For example, some programs review and revise course materials and syllabi on a regular basis. The online component can be assessed and edited for accessibility at the same time content is reviewed. Another option is to develop a schedule for reviewing and revising existing online courses a few at a time, beginning with the most frequently offered courses or the courses with the highest enrollment, since these courses are most likely to have a student with a disability enrolled in them. Some established courses take more time and effort to revise than others, but planning ahead allows the time necessary to create effective and accessible materials.

Content Management Systems

Many colleges and universities use a learning management system (LMS) to manage their online courses or as a supplement to face-to-face courses. This software provides structure and tools such as bulletin boards, mail, chat rooms, online quizzes and tests, a way to submit homework assignments, and file storage. Typically the LMS provides a general template, and faculty members add their specific course content to it.

All of the major LMSs make an effort toward accessibility, though some are more successful than others, and none of them are perfect. However, even if completely accessible LMSs were available, the instructors' materials must also be created with accessibility in mind. An accessible LMS will be rendered inaccessible if the instructor adds inaccessible materials to the course, such as poorly formatted documents or uncaptioned videos.

It is important for instructors to make their materials and course components as accessible as possible. However, no matter how much effort they put into considering all of the obstacles students may face and trying to make everything accessible, it is impossible to guarantee complete accessibility. Sometimes an additional accommodation must be made on a case-by-case basis. Nevertheless, careful planning and good design will decrease the number of individual accommodations that must be made.

Accessibility Versus Usability

Instructors should keep the difference between accessibility and usability in mind. While accessibility is the baseline, usability is the real goal. Whenever possible, students with disabilities should be able to use materials with the same amount of effort as students without disabilities.

With the rationale for providing accessible materials established, we address the details of how to accomplish this goal.

Word Processing Documents. For the most part, documents that are created using a word processing program are accessible. Nevertheless, several techniques can be implemented to increase usability.

Whenever available, the formatting tools that the word processing software provides should be used. For example, if there is a tool to mark text as a title or a heading, it should be used instead of changing the font or type size manually to visually denote a title. These software tools produce a hidden code that can be read by assistive technology to let students know they are reading a title or section heading, but assistive technology does not inform the reader that a title has been introduced when large, bold type is simply used.

Table and columns creation tools are available in most word processors and should be used instead of the tab key or space bar to line up columns. Again, hidden code makes tables and columns easier to read by text-to-speech software.

Pictures or images in the text need to have alternative text. Alternative text, sometimes referred to as ALT-text, is a brief description of the picture that text-to-speech software programs read. The text should explain the important aspects of the image to someone who cannot see it. Alternative text can usually be added in the image properties section. If the word processor does not have the option to add alternative text to the image, a text caption can be added underneath the picture instead.

Text boxes should be avoided whenever possible because text-to-speech software generally cannot read it.

Scanned Documents. Documents that have been scanned are a frequent problem for accessibility and usability. Unless the scanned file has been run through optical character recognition (OCR) software, it is likely only a picture of words, not readable text. Text-to-speech software cannot recognize the pictures as words and therefore cannot read the words aloud to students who cannot see them or need auditory access to the content because of reading difficulties.

With advanced planning, OCR software can be used with the document to make it accessible. The OCR software scans the pictures of words and tries to recognize patterns of lines that form letters. Using OCR requires some training with specialized software, and the results should be manually proofread for accuracy. A campus that uses many scanned documents may decide to invest in high-quality OCR software that has better character recognition than lower-cost or free versions. For cost-effectiveness and efficiency, a campus may have a centralized point for document conversion with high-quality software and trained staff who can convert documents for the entire campus or university. Foresight allows for a less hectic and productive start to a semester for faculty, staff, and students.

Slide Presentations. Slide presentations are popular for live lectures. Many instructors who start teaching a course online after having taught it face-to-face put slide presentations from their face-to-face courses online without adaptation or consideration of whether the slide presentation is the optimal way to present the information. Often slide presentations are intended to be accompanied by a live speaker and are less effective when presented alone unless they have been adapted for online use.

Although it is possible to create slide presentations that are effective for online courses, making an accessible slide presentation is much more difficult. Initially instructors should decide whether the slide presentation is used because it serves a purpose or if it is just a carryover from the face-to-face version of the course. If it is the latter, another format may serve the same purpose more effectively and more accessibly. Whenever possible, documents should be created in a format that is accessible for all students.

Some steps can be taken to improve the accessibility of a slide presentation. For example, using plain text and avoiding images, graphs, and charts will make a presentation more accessible. Necessary images can be described in the notes section of the slide. However, these techniques will not guarantee access because students use a variety of assistive technologies. The best and simplest way to provide access is to have an additional text-only equivalent of the information in the presentation.

The text-only equivalent is easy to produce by copying the text from the slide presentation into a word processing document and providing text equivalents of any pictures, charts, or graphs from the slides. Slide numbers added at appropriate places in the text can help students follow along and find specific places in the text easily. Both the slide presentation and the text equivalent should be made available to all students so they can choose their preferred file format.

Audio and Video. Audio and video can add depth and interest to an online course and can benefit many students with disabilities. Video should be used only if the video adds more to the course content than audio alone. Demonstrating a technique or showing archival footage are examples of using video well. A video of the professor talking in front of the camera, also known as a talking head, is not a good use of video. Video files are larger than audio files, meaning they take up more disk space and require more time for students to download. They are also more difficult and expensive to make accessible. Video should therefore be used judiciously.

A transcript (that is, a verbatim script of the audio content) of audio files is required to make them accessible. Transcripts benefit students with hearing loss. They are also appreciated by second-language learners and by all students when the speaker has a strong accent. Transcripts also serve as useful study tools for all students.

Many agencies are available to transcribe audio, but transcripts also can be created by student workers because little special training and few skills are necessary beyond attention to detail and good typing skills. The transcript should be provided at the same time the audio is made available.

For video, providing a simple transcript of the audio track is not sufficient. The text must be synchronized with the video using captions. There are two types of captions: open and closed. Open captions are part of the video itself and will always be visible. Closed captions can be turned on and off through the software used to play the video. Either option provides accessibility as long as students know how to turn the captions on and off for closed captions. Because transcripts provide additional benefits for all students, the instructor may choose to make transcripts available in addition to captions, but it is not generally required.

Audio descriptions of videos are necessary for students who are blind or have low vision and cannot see the action on the screen. In some videos, a speaker or narrator may describe enough of the action that no further description is needed. If all important information cannot be gleaned by just listening to the sound, audio descriptions will need to be added.

Although transcripts can be easily done in-house, synchronizing captions and creating audio descriptions require more training and more specialized software, and should probably be outsourced. The chapter appendix provides URLs for information on finding an agency to caption or create audio descriptions for video.

Chat Rooms. Chat rooms can help replicate the energy of face-to-face classroom discussions. Students receive immediate feedback from the instructor and other students without waiting for a discussion board post or e-mail. They may also feel that they get to know each other better because the feedback seems like a natural discussion. However, chat rooms can pose problems for some students with disabilities.

Text-to-speech software that many students who are blind use may not work with some chat rooms, depending on the software used. Even if the software is able to read the text in the chat window, listening to text read aloud is slower than reading silently. It may be difficult for blind students to keep up with a live chat room conversation.

Students who cannot use their arms or hands or have poor fine motor skills will also have difficulty with chat rooms. Online conversations tend to move quickly. Students may be able to type with time and effort, but the topics will likely shift before students can type their question or comment.

Some students with learning disabilities, hearing loss, or cognitive disabilities read slowly or need additional time to gather and compose their thoughts before responding. The fast pace of chat rooms may give them little time to read and respond before the conversation scrolls off the screen or moves to another topic. Students with disabilities who have poor spelling and grammar skills may be inhibited or embarrassed about typing mistakes and may avoid participating in the chat conversation.

Students with attention deficit disorder (with or without hyperactivity) may have problems maintaining focus. If they are distracted by something else in their environment, they will miss conversations that took place while they looked away from the screen. They may also have difficulty refocusing after a distraction.

But in spite of the difficulties for some students, chat rooms are a useful tool for online learning. One way to make chat rooms easier for students with disabilities is to have a moderator who controls the pace of the conversation. In some chat room programs, participants can press a button to indicate they want to make a comment or ask a question. The moderator can see which students have virtually raised their hands and call on them individually, making sure that each student has a chance to participate and time to type comments. This technique slows the pace of the conversation and provides access to students who need more time to read and respond.

If the chat system within the LMS does not meet the accessibility needs of students with disabilities in the course, other options for real-time interaction may be explored. Chat systems written in HTML and some instant messaging programs are more accessible to text-to-speech software.

Audio chats are another option, making it easier for students who have difficulty reading or typing. However, audio chat tools have problems of their own. Students with hearing loss will not be able to easily participate in audio chats. They are also difficult for students with speech impediments, auditory processing disorders, or cognitive disabilities who need more time than usual to process information.

Unfortunately there is no one-size-fits-all chat room option to date. The approach selected should be determined by the specific types of disabilities the students in the class have. As a result, techniques may differ from semester to semester, depending on the needs of the students enrolled. In the case of chat rooms, finding a universal design approach may not be possible.

As a last resort, chat logs or transcripts can be provided for those who cannot participate. Most chat room software can keep a transcript of the conversation, and those logs are generally easy for the instructor to obtain and make available to students. Although participation in the live chat is preferred, transcripts of the conversation can provide students with the information discussed. In addition, students who read more slowly or are distractible will appreciate the ability to review information they may have missed, and the transcript can serve as a reference for all students.

Quizzes and Tests. Extra time on quizzes and tests is a common accommodation for students with disabilities. Most LMSs provide a way to create a duplicate test with a different time limit. The permissions for the test can be set so that students who need extra time see one test while the rest of the class sees the other.

General Web Accessibility

The recommendations addressed so far are specific to online courses, especially those managed by an LMS. But some instructors create a Web site for their course instead of, or in addition to, the LMS. This section provides general guidelines for Web accessibility. A Web designer or someone from the information technology support office may need to implement some of these features, but instructors who are aware of issues can bring them to the attention of appropriate staff.

Alternative Text. Alternative text is a brief description of a picture that can be seen by text-to-speech software and read aloud to students who cannot see the picture. When a mouse is rolled over a picture on a site, a text box should appear displaying the alternative text of that picture. If the text box does not appear, images can be turned off in the browser options, causing the text to display where the pictures normally appear. If the text says something uninformative such as "pic000123.jpg" or "Picture 1," consider the purpose of the picture. Determine the critical information that the picture conveys and how that information can be expressed in one or two short sentences. The alternative text should be changed to reflect the picture's purpose.

Also look for words that are actually images. For example, the button that returns students to the home page may be a picture of the word "Home" instead of text. The alternative text should match the displayed word exactly (that is, "Home," not "Picture of the word Home").

Use of Color. While color can be used to help convey information, students who are blind or color blind cannot see the colors, so the information must be delivered in another way. For example, a form that has required information indicated in red could also have an asterisk by those items. A green button that starts an exercise could also be labeled "Start."

High color contrast between the text and the background is important for easy readability. Achieving this is more difficult than it sounds because some color combinations that appear to have high contrast to someone with typical vision may not be clear to someone with low vision or color blindness. The appendix at the end of this chapter has links to sites that can mimic different types of color blindness and suggest color combinations for high contrast. Also, avoid all patterned backgrounds because the clutter greatly reduces contrast. A simple test for contrast is to print out the page on a black and white printer and then make several generations of photocopies. If the text becomes difficult to read after a few copies, the contrast may not be high enough.

Data Tables. Similar to tables in word processing documents, the tools available for creating tables and charts on Web pages should be used instead of the tab key or space bar. Tables should be used to convey information, not to format the layout of the page. A good general rule of thumb is to use software tools for their intended purpose whenever they are available.

The first row or column of a chart or table can be used to provide headings to indicate the content of each row or column. For example, a person with typical vision can easily glance at a chart and see that it is a mailing list with names, addresses, and phone numbers. It is much more difficult for someone with impaired vision. Adding a heading to each column that says "Name," "Address," and "Phone" makes the chart easier for a person who is blind to understand and navigate. A Web designer can add code to make charts and tables even more accessible, but adding headings can usually be done easily when the chart or table is created.

Forms. A Web designer will need to add specific code to make forms accessible, but some simple techniques can be done by anyone using Web page creation software. For example, required fields on a form should be identified by an asterisk or the word *required* in parentheses after the label, not by visual cues such as color, italics, or bold type. Another technique is to provide the description of information to be entered before the entry box, not after. For example, the form should say "Name" followed by the space to type the name, not the reverse.

To determine the order in which the form will be read by text-to-speech software, start at the top and press the tab key repeatedly to move through the form. If the cursor does not progress in a logical manner, a Web designer can adjust the form. Some forms, such as log-in screens, have a time limit in which the information must be entered. A Web designer can add an option to request extra time to allow a person who types slowly the opportunity to enter the required information.

Drop-Down Menus. Drop-down menus need to have a Go or Submit button for students to press after highlighting their choice. Drop-down menus that automatically send users to the highlighted location when the mouse button is released cause problems for students using text-to-speech software. Their software automatically takes them to the first option before having an opportunity to hear the other choices.

Link Names. In the early days of the Internet, almost every link said "click here." Today assistive technology allows students with disabilities to pull up a list of all the links on the page, allowing them to find a link quickly and easily. Unfortunately, a list of links that all say "click here" is not informative. A better practice is to make the link descriptive of the destination, such as "Home," "Apply for Admission," or "Contact Us."

Navigation. Starting at the top of the page and pressing the tab key moves the cursor through the page in the order that text-to-speech software will read the page. If the cursor does not move in a logical order, a Web designer may need to adjust the layout so the text-to-speech software will present the page in a more useful manner. If the navigation links are the same on every page, there should be a link at the top of the page that jumps directly to the main content. By clicking on this link, a student using text-to-speech software can avoid listening to the same menu again and again on each new page.

Mouse Dependency. Some students with disabilities are unable to use a mouse to navigate the computer screen. This may be because they cannot see the screen or do not have the physical ability to control the mouse. Students must be able to navigate and use the Web site with just the keyboard. Some pages use mouse-over links that show additional choices when the cursor is placed over a menu item. These types of menus should be avoided, or duplicate links should be placed elsewhere on the page.

Conclusion

Implementing these accessibility features when designing online courses saves time, money, and stress and benefits all students. Most of the techniques for adapting materials are simple to use, and even many people without much computer experience can do them. Although nothing will guarantee complete accessibility to all potential students, advance planning will reduce the number of individual accommodations needed when a student with a disability takes an online course.

Appendix: Additional Resources

Because Web addresses may change, a current and more extensive list of resources can be found at http://www.bethcase.com.

Captions and Audio Description for Video

Described and Captioned Media Program, http://www.dcmp.org /About/Vendors/Default.aspx

Color Use

AccessColor, http://www.accesskeys.org/tools/color-contrast.html
Lighthouse International, http://www.lighthouse.org/accessibility
    /effective-color-contrast/

General Web Accessibility

Web Accessibility Initiative, http://www.w3.org/WAI
WebAIM (Web Accessibility in Mind), http://www.webaim.org

Legal

Section 508.gov, http://www.section508.gov
United States Access Board, http://www.access-board.gov

Software Accessibility

Accessibility in Microsoft Products, http://www.microsoft.com/enable
    /products
Adobe Accessibility Resource Center, http://www.adobe.com
    /accessibility

References

Allen, I. E., and Seaman, J. 2010. "Learning on Demand: Online Education in the
    United States." 2009. Retrieved July 26, 2010, from http://www.sloanconsortium.org
    /publications/survey/pdf/learningondemand.pdf.
Americans with Disabilities Act of 1990, 42 U.S.C.A. § 12101 et seq. 1990. Retrieved
    July 28, 2010, from http://www.ada.gov/statute.html.
Coombs, N. "Transcending Distances and Differences." *AAHE Bulletin*, 2000, *53*(2), 3–5.
Fichten, C. S., Ferraro, V., Asuncion, J.V., Chwojka, C., Barile, M., Nguyen, M.N.,
    Klomp, R., and Wolforth, J. "Disabilities and e-Learning Problems and Solutions: An
    Exploratory Study." *Educational Technology & Society*, 2009, *12*(4), 241–256.
Higher Education Opportunity Act. U.S. Code. Title 20, §§ 1001 note. 2008.
Kinash, S., Crichton, S., and Kim-Rupnow, W. S. "A Review of 2000-2003 Literature at
    the Intersection of Online Learning and Disability." *American Journal of Distance Edu-
    cation*, 2004, *18*(1), 5–19.
Parsad, B., and Lewis, L. *Distance Education at Degree-Granting Postsecondary Institu-
    tions: 2006–07*. Washington, D.C.: National Center for Education Statistics, Institute
    of Education Sciences, U.S. Department of Education, 2008.
Parton, B. S., Hancock, R. J., and Oescher, J. 2009. "An Examination of Web Content
    Accessibility Guidelines Compliance: Are Universities and School Districts Making
    World Wide Web Learning Resources Available to the Disabled?" In *Research High-
    lights in Technology and Teacher Education*, edited by Cleborne D. Maddux, 257–264.
    Chesapeake, VA: Society for Information Technology & Teacher Education (SITE).
Rowland, C. "Accessibility of the Internet in Postsecondary Education: Meeting the
    Challenge." Paper presented at the Universal Web Accessibility Symposium 2000, San
    Antonio, Tex., Oct. 2000.

U.S. Government Accountability Office. *Higher Education and Disability: Education Needs a Coordinated Approach to Improve Its Assistance to Schools in Supporting Students*. Report to the Chairman, Committee on Education and Labor, House of Representatives, Oct. 2009.

Vocational Rehabilitation Act. P.L. 93–112, U.S. Code. Vol. 29, § 701 et seq., 1973.

Vocational Rehabilitation Amendments. P.L. 105-220, U.S. Code. Vol. 29, § 794d, 1998.

D. ELIZABETH CASE *is working toward a doctorate in instructional technology at Texas Tech University in Lubbock, Texas.*

ROSEANNA C. DAVIDSON *is an associate professor of special education at Texas Tech University in Lubbock, Texas.*

NEW DIRECTIONS FOR STUDENT SERVICES • DOI: 10.1002/ss

6

This chapter focuses on the key support services and advising procedures that institutions of higher education should have in place for students with disabilities as they participate in education abroad opportunities.

Education Abroad for Students with Disabilities: Expanding Access

Heidi M. Soneson, Shelly Fisher

Education abroad is a rapidly expanding opportunity for undergraduate students in the United States. According to statistics prepared annually by the Institute on International Education, the number of students studying abroad from the United States exceeded 260,000 in 2008-2009. Not only are U.S. and overseas institutions diversifying the number and variety of education abroad opportunities available to students, but many departments at U.S. institutions of higher education are strongly encouraging and even requiring overseas experience as part of a student's degree program.

Concurrent with this growth in total numbers is a growth in the diversity of participants. Students with different ethnic backgrounds, academic majors, age, socioeconomic status, and disabilities are increasingly seeking opportunities overseas. In order to provide effective support to this expanding group of participants, administrative offices across campus need to coordinate support services and design effective advising procedures. The responsibility cannot and should not lie solely with the education abroad office on campus. It is the combined expertise of the various units on campus, academic and administrative, that will enable students to realize their academic goals, including an education abroad experience.

This chapter focuses on the key support services and advising procedures that institutions of higher education should have in place in order to guide students with disabilities as they explore and participate in education abroad opportunities. The eight themes that this chapter explores provide both theoretical considerations and practical suggestions or resources for student services offices to consider when guiding students with disabilities.

NEW DIRECTIONS FOR STUDENT SERVICES, no. 134, Summer 2011 © Wiley Periodicals, Inc.
Published online in Wiley Online Library (wileyonlinelibrary.com) • DOI: 10.1002/ss.395

A summary list of key resources is provided in the chapter appendix for convenient future reference. We recognize that resources and student needs fluctuate and hope that the information contained in this chapter serves as a foundation for effective support through changing times.

A Comprehensive Advising Approach

The advising process for students with disabilities who wish to study abroad requires a collaborative approach. Although education abroad offices are the experts on specific program options, they are frequently not familiar with the range of disability accommodations that a student might need on campus and perhaps abroad. Guidance regarding financial support for education abroad opportunities often rests with multiple offices, including the office for financial aid, the disability services office, the education abroad office, and even the student's academic department. In addition, the ability of a student to take a reduced course load while overseas or to take one or more classes on a pass/fail basis, for example, as part of a disability accommodation, will require the coordination of various advisors on campus and overseas. In order to serve students with disabilities successfully, it is important to establish clear areas of expertise among relevant offices, as well as designated contact people in each office to assist with questions as they arise. It is particularly important that advisors recognize the limits of their expertise in order to avoid the possibility that a student receives inappropriate or insufficient disability accommodations.

The following guidelines can help key offices define areas of expertise:

Education-Abroad Office

- Provide information on education abroad opportunities.
- Collect information on disability accommodations at popular overseas programs.
- Work with overseas colleagues or program providers to understand general attitudes toward individuals with disabilities at popular overseas locations.
- Foster disclosure through print and Web images and statements.
- Work with the disability services office to develop advising materials for students with disabilities.
- Receive training from the disability services office staff on working with students with disabilities.
- Foster disclosure of a student's disability accommodation needs as part of the post-acceptance process, which is then shared with the disability services office.
- Work with the disability services office to clarify whether requested accommodations are possible on particular education abroad programs.

- Provide resources on cultural perceptions of disability and level of support services that exist overseas.

Disability Services Office

- Provide training to the education abroad office staff on the range of disabilities (visual and hidden) occurring on campus and examples of typical on-campus accommodations.
- Review disability accommodation requests from students with disabilities wishing to study abroad and clarify for the education abroad office the essential accommodations that particular students need.
- Distribute education abroad advising materials, and underscore for students the importance of early accommodation disclosure.
- Advise on financial resources available to assist students in overseas accommodations.
- Provide a link from the disability services Web site to the education abroad Web site in order to foster shared and collaborative advising services.

Financial Aid Office

- Provide advice on general financial support for students.
- Consult with the education abroad office to clarify the kinds of financial support that can be applied to education abroad opportunities.
- Clarify with disability services any restrictions on applying accommodation support funds toward education abroad costs.

Academic Advising Offices

- Clarify any impact a particular academic accommodation might have on a student's academic program, including taking a reduced course load or the option to take one or more classes on a pass-or-fail basis.
- Encourage students to disclose any disability needs early to the education abroad office so that appropriate accommodations can be discussed well in advance.

Counseling and Health Services

- Advise student on ways to continue necessary medication overseas, including dosage, supply, and whether adjustments may be needed given the overseas context.
- Review any required immunizations and any possible impact of specific immunizations on the student's current health or the student's current medication.

NEW DIRECTIONS FOR STUDENT SERVICES • DOI: 10.1002/ss

- Consult with the student about possible counseling services that he or she might need overseas or technological options for continuing counseling with a U.S. counselor while abroad.

Additional offices on campus can play a critical role in advising students with disabilities. These include support offices for students of color, the women's center, legal counsel, as well as support offices for gay, lesbian, bisexual, and transgender students. In each case, it is critical to establish procedures for coordination and to identify contact people in each office to foster communication when particular questions arise.

We recommend that the education abroad office and other support offices publish procedures on their office Web pages or in advising handbooks so that students with disabilities clearly understand where to turn for the advice they need.

Creating a Welcome Environment

Creating a welcoming environment is central to fostering disclosure and trust among students with disabilities who are pursuing education abroad opportunities. Early disclosure allows the student, the education abroad office, disability services, and all other support units on campus to provide interested students with comprehensive and timely advice and guidance. A welcoming environment is best achieved in three key areas: staff training, Web and other visual materials, and the physical office environment.

Staff Training. Although each office has specific areas of expertise, some cross-training allows each office to provide initial support and guidance to students with disabilities. In particular, annual training meetings between the disability services office and the education abroad office not only benefit students with disabilities seeking advice on overseas study opportunities but also provide office staff with the opportunity to expand their knowledge, understanding, and professional expertise, as well as form important collegial relationships with the other office. A number of topics are germane to this discussion:

- An ice-breaker activity that allows staff across offices to meet each other and learn about the other person's expertise.
- An introduction to the different kinds of disabilities and examples of typical on-campus accommodations.
- Tips for successful advising: Should you offer to guide a blind person who enters your office? How much background information do you need to know about a person's disability? How is it best to ask about a student's disability needs?
- Case scenarios to illustrate and discuss specific advising situations.
- An overview of the education abroad options that are available to students.

- Examples of past student experiences and what can be learned from these examples.
- A review of key advising materials and whether they meet current student needs.
- Steps that should be taken if a student needs education abroad materials translated into Braille or requires a reader.
- Communication procedures for students and office staff. Should students ask for a specific person in the education abroad or disability services office? Should staff have one specific contact person in each office for all questions, or is a different structure preferred?

Formal annual meetings should be complemented by more informal communication. Taking the time to call a colleague at the other office or exchange e-mails about a particular student to clarify next steps helps build good working relationships that in turn help provide a well-coordinated advising process for the student.

Web and Other Outreach Materials. Students are more likely to feel supported and welcomed if they can see themselves in the visual images an office displays. This includes information produced for an office's Web site, promotional brochures and featured stories, and images displayed in the office. Images of students with disabilities in overseas settings can help students begin to see themselves in the new context. Images that include geographical locations to help give a sense of a country's particular environment or images that are accompanied by text or quotations encouraging students with disabilities to consider study abroad and to disclose their needs early are important steps for a comprehensive advising approach.

The Physical Office Environment. Education abroad offices should request an assessment of their physical space and signage to determine what steps could be taken to help facilitate access for students with disabilities. Having office signage in Braille or program materials at a height accessible for students in wheelchairs is an important accommodation. Movable furniture might also be arranged in such a way that students with physical disabilities can more easily use the space offered for advising or to use the office resource library. In many cases, these accommodations do not necessarily require significant expense and can be of great assistance to students with disabilities who visit the advising office.

Specific Advising Strategies

Education abroad and disability services offices should determine and document how students with disabilities can best assess whether and which education abroad opportunities are workable for them. Both Web-based advising steps and written materials should be easily accessible in both

offices and, potentially, other key offices on campus. Although every institution of higher education has its own specific program selection procedures, the following general guidelines can be helpful to students with
disabilities:

- Select a range of programs to maximize the possibility of finding
  one that can accommodate a particular disability accommodation
  request.
- Identify programs and disclose disability needs at least two months
  prior to the application deadline date so that there is sufficient time
  to investigate accommodation possibilities.
- Meet with a disability services advisor to discuss accommodation
  needs and disclose these to the education abroad office.
- Determine in consultation with the education abroad office what
  accommodations are possible overseas.
- Investigate scholarships or other forms of financial support.
- Explore what kinds of disability support systems or offices exist in
  the countries of interest.
- Contact other students with disabilities who have studied abroad to
  learn about their experiences.

Accommodation Requests

One of the most important steps in assisting students with disabilities in
their education abroad selection process is to provide a comprehensive
method for determining a student's disability need and help the student
anticipate what accommodations might be necessary overseas, including
those they may not currently use at home. Although general information
can be identified in a health or disability disclosure form, it is best to have
a more detailed accommodation request form available for students to complete after their initial disclosure. In some cases, further, or perhaps even
initial, disclosure may occur overseas. Recommended predeparture procedures and on-site procedures are discussed in further detail below.
     While in the United States. A general health or disability disclosure
form is an excellent initial way to gather basic information on a student's
disability needs. The health and disability information may be contained on
the same form or as separate forms. In order to encourage disability
disclosure, it is helpful to include a brief explanation to the student to
indicate that the information will remain private and will be used to
identify necessary accommodations to facilitate sufficient support while the
student is overseas. The importance of disclosure should be reinforced in
other program materials such as brochures and predeparture handbooks
and at orientation.
     This information should always be collected after a student's acceptance
into a particular program. Collecting this information prior to acceptance

inhibits disclosure and can run the risk of appearing to be discriminatory against certain types of students. If there are concerns about accepting a student due to a particular disability accommodation need, the program acceptance letter or release and waiver form can stipulate that students must be able to participate in the essential aspects of the program. It is best to consult with legal counsel to determine what wording is appropriate at your particular institution.

Once a student has established initial disability needs, he or she should be asked to complete a more detailed form outlining possible accommodation needs in the classroom, in housing, and on excursions. The student should complete the form with the assistance of the campus disability services office so that there is a dialogue between the student and the disability services advisor regarding the range of possible needs abroad. The completed form should be submitted to the education abroad office to review. In some cases, a meeting with the education abroad advisor, the student, and the disability services advisor is helpful to discuss a student's particular needs.

This information should then be shared with the overseas staff to determine what accommodations might be possible. The accommodations request form should provide space for the overseas staff to clarify what accommodations might be possible in each area where an accommodation need is documented. This information should be conveyed to the student and the student's disability services advisor in writing or by e-mail; an in-person meeting may also be helpful.

It is not unusual for additional conversation and correspondence to take place among all parties as the realities of the overseas site are considered in combination with the needs of the student. In some cases, the student and disability services office may want to do additional research through contact with disability organizations in the destination location to assist in identifying other accommodation resources to suggest. It may be determined that the overseas site cannot provide the necessary accommodations. In other cases, some or all of the accommodation needs can be provided. The decision as to whether a particular program can provide the necessary accommodations to ensure that the student can participate in the essential aspects of the overseas program will be a joint one among all parties.

When establishing whether an overseas program can provide the necessary accommodations, the following considerations should be kept in mind:

- Not all overseas staff have experience working with students with disabilities or assessing accommodation needs. It is important to encourage overseas colleagues to be honest in their assessment of their overseas support possibilities, but it is also important to encourage connection with disability offices or organizations in

NEW DIRECTIONS FOR STUDENT SERVICES • DOI: 10.1002/ss

their country to learn what is available and to engage in creative problem solving. Can a standard excursion take place in a new location to offer greater accessibility? Could the student with a disability accommodation request an alternative activity that is accessible?

- Many accommodations do not require significant expense or substantial alterations to an overseas location. Accommodations such as extra time on tests, the ability to sit at the front of the classroom in order to see the board, or a request to borrow class notes from other students requires little or no cost to the overseas site. Once a student discloses an accommodation need, it is helpful for the education abroad office to discuss typical accommodation requests with the disability services office and convey these suggestions to the overseas site.

- A review of disability accommodation requests should identify what constitutes the essential aspects of a particular program. For some programs, access to the academic program is most important, and cocurricular activities may be varied and flexible. For other programs, planned excursions or other activities may be an integral part of the program, and the overseas staff will need to consider how required program activities can address a student's accommodation request without fundamentally altering the activity. If the student will not be able to participate in the essential aspects of the program, it is best to assist him or her in identifying a different education abroad program. In some cases, it may not be possible to identify a program that meets the student's academic, personal, and disability accommodation needs. In these cases, it is important to establish with legal counsel the institutional expectations and criteria for providing accommodations.

- Education abroad offices should collect information on general disability accommodation possibilities for popular sites and provide this information in advising materials to assist students with disabilities in their selection process. Although disability needs vary with each student, general information on an overseas country's approach to individuals with disabilities and more detailed information on the accessibility of a particular site can help students consider their options well in advance. It also provides an opportunity for program staff to discuss general accommodation possibilities with overseas sites and enlist ideas from the disability services office in order to have helpful information available. In some cases, overseas sites may be able to access support from local disability service offices if these links can be explored before a participating student arrives. It is important to note the date when the information was collected because accessibility information for a given location can become out of date relatively quickly.

Once Overseas. Because students with disabilities generally require continued support while overseas, it is important that the overseas staff identify a disability-related contact person for the student who can offer support to the student on arrival at the site. In some cases, a student may require additional services once overseas. In rare circumstances, the student may disclose a disability need only once he or she has arrived overseas. In these cases, the overseas site should consult with the U.S. program provider and the student's U.S. disability services advisor to discuss what accommodations are feasible and appropriate. Although an overseas program is not required to provide disability accommodations on short notice, many accommodations do not require significant expense or staff time.

In both the United States and overseas, privacy is important. Staff should carefully consider who needs to know about a particular student's disability needs and discuss with the student who will be informed about any accommodation needs so that the student is aware of those who can provide support.

Preparing Students for the Experience

Helping students prepare for their experience overseas is a critical step in the predeparture process. The following considerations are useful topics to share with students with disabilities in order to assist them with their general predeparture preparations and, specifically, with the differences in the approach to disabilities that they may experience while overseas.

Cross-Cultural Considerations. Intercultural experiences can be intense emotional experiences for everyone. Students should be encouraged to remember this and consider that in order to develop intercultural sensitivity, one must have such challenging experiences. That said, in addition to considering what types of accommodations are available to students with disabilities at different sites abroad, advisors should also discuss with students how they plan to interact with the local community. Do they want to live with a host family, or would they be more comfortable living with other students? Would they like those students to be from the host country or from the United States? Does the student prefer to take classes with other U.S. students or with local and international students? Does the student understand the host country's classroom norms and grading system, and is he or she comfortable with it? Students with disabilities should specifically consider how different cultural norms in that country might affect how host country nationals perceive and receive them.

Although simply studying in another country is important for culture learning and intercultural development, it is no longer thought to be sufficient for students on education abroad programs. Guided reflection is a valuable addition to the process of learning in and out of the classroom and

NEW DIRECTIONS FOR STUDENT SERVICES • DOI: 10.1002/ss

one that should begin prior to students' departure. Advisors will need to strike a balance between the cultural preparation that all students going abroad should consider and the additional points involved when understanding disabilities from another culture's perspective. Here are some suggestions for students:

- Learn how people with disabilities are viewed in the country to which you will be going.
- Recognize that people with disabilities may have different norms and accommodations in different cultures. For example, people may have a different idea of independence than students are used to and may "help" without asking first.
- Take time to think about your goals for the period you will be abroad, and devise a plan for achieving those goals. Revisit this list frequently while you are abroad, and reassess if necessary.
- Consider how you self-identify, and then consider how someone in your host country who is meeting you for the first time would identify you. Then consider the inverse: How are you identifying someone you meet for the first time in relation to how this person would describe himself or herself?
- Honor the Platinum Rule: Treat others not as you would like to be treated, but as they would like to be treated.
- Remember to communicate with members of the local community while you are abroad, so you can talk about experiences that you find confusing or frustrating.

Predeparture Preparations. A checklist can be helpful for assisting students with their preparations for an education abroad experience. Although many items on the list are common to all students, a few can be of particular assistance to students with disabilities. The following suggestions are helpful to include:

- Discuss medication needs with your physician and disability services. It is generally illegal to ship medication overseas, and it is thus important to clarify what medication you will need to bring with you. If any medication might need to be filled overseas, consult with your U.S. physician and your program's international insurance company about whether the medication and its dosage are available overseas.
- Meet with the appropriate campus offices regarding any scholarships, loans, or other financial support that might be dedicated to disability needs. Ensure that these funds will be available to you if you plan to use them toward overseas costs.
- If possible, talk with other students with disabilities who have studied abroad about their experiences.

NEW DIRECTIONS FOR STUDENT SERVICES • DOI: 10.1002/ss

- Research disability services offices or organizations that might exist in the country where you will be studying to learn what support they may be able to provide.
- Confirm with the education abroad office the accommodations that you will receive, and be certain to identify your on-site contact so that you know to whom to turn to discuss your accommodation needs while overseas.
- If you plan to travel during your stay abroad, investigate any accommodation needs in advance, including flight or other transportation accommodations.
- Be certain to identify how to correspond with your disability services specialist once you are overseas, in case you wish to discuss any needs you may have. The disability services advisor, the education abroad advisor, and the overseas staff will consider together what accommodations are possible.

Financial Considerations

Should a student's disability accommodation request involve costs overseas, institutions should consult with their legal counsel. Although no national or international case law requires U.S. institutions of higher education to provide overseas accommodations to students with disabilities, these institutions should consider it part of their institutional mission to assist all students in accessing international educational opportunities to the fullest extent possible and reasonable.

If cost is involved in enabling a student with a disability to participate in a particular overseas program, each institution needs to determine how to respond. In some cases, the disability services office may have a source of funds for particular overseas accommodations, such as hiring a tutor or reader. In other cases, the education abroad office, program provider, or even an institution's central administration may have funds available to modify its overseas site. If this modification could also benefit future students (such as installing a ramp to access an overseas program office or purchasing movable chairs in a classroom), the program provider should consider whether to make the investment for the benefit of all students. This is in keeping with the principles of universal design, an approach to access that is widespread at U.S. institutions of higher education in the United States, and it should be applied overseas whenever possible.

Depending on the particular disability accommodation need and each institution's financial resources and policy decisions regarding education abroad, some costs may be the responsibility of the student. Transportation for free-time activities, bringing a dedicated companion to assist with daily needs, particular technology needs specifically designed for that student, or additional costs associated with travel from the housing location to the classroom may be the student's responsibility. Each institution needs to assess

NEW DIRECTIONS FOR STUDENT SERVICES • DOI: 10.1002/ss

with its office of the general counsel what guidelines to establish regarding institutional responsibility for overseas disability accommodations.

Administrative Considerations

When developing a relationship with overseas institutions, whether to establish an exchange program, host a short-term faculty-led program, or develop institutional linkages on several levels, U.S. institutions should incorporate language regarding equal access into their partnership agreements. Including statements that indicate that both the U.S. and the overseas institution are committed to equal access for all students will help create a supportive atmosphere in which discussions regarding specific student needs can take place. Although an overseas site may not be able to accommodate a particular disability request, it is important to have a general discussion at the start of a new partnership to clarify the importance of providing equal access to all students—those with and without disabilities—and to confirm the nature of the administrative support at both institutions.

Considerations on Return

Reentry can be more challenging for students than their time abroad. Predeparture preparation and orientations at the beginning of their programs may overlook information on processing the return home. While students have had new and exciting experiences while abroad, their friends and family have also moved ahead with their lives.

Some students will feel a sense of relief to come home. It will be a chance to return to family and friends and possibly a more accessible life. Other students will feel sadness about leaving their host site. They may relish the new sense of independence they developed while abroad, and some may have enjoyed greater accommodation and more positive social interactions at the host site than at home.

Prior to their departure from the education abroad site, students should be encouraged to think about how they will say goodbye to their home abroad and what they envision for their return home.

The majority of students who return from an education abroad experience, including those with disabilities, report an increase in independence, self-awareness, resilience, appreciation of differences, and comfort with ambiguity. This growth contributes to the desired personal development outcomes of education abroad offices and institutions of higher education and is a necessary step toward building intercultural sensitivity development. Here are some practical suggestions:

- Ask students with disabilities who return from an education abroad experience to provide tips and suggestions to include on the education abroad office's Web site for future students.

- Invite returning students with disabilities to submit photos and comments in order to create a more diverse and comprehensive image of education abroad students in visual materials.
- Develop a brief survey to capture the student's experience overseas and impression of disability access at the overseas site that can be summarized on the education abroad office's Web site or included with advising materials.
- If a university or regional group of universities and colleges offers a reentry event or conference, invite students with disabilities to attend, debrief their experiences abroad, and learn how to parlay those events into transferable skills for employers, graduate schools, and their own personal lives as engaged participants of the world.
- If the education abroad office has returned students give short presentations to classes across campus, encourage students with disabilities to participate. Hearing from a student with a disability may prompt another student with a disability to consider something he or she once thought was impossible.
- Suggest that returned students get involved with activities organized by the international students and scholars office, for example, by participating in social activities or becoming a language partner.

Appendix: Critical Resources

A number of resources exist to assist offices in developing advising materials to support students with disabilities who are exploring education abroad opportunities. After each Web site listed, a short description outlines the resources that can be found on that particular site at the time of this publication:

Access Abroad

The University of Minnesota received federal funding to establish a Web site and advising tools dedicated to students with disabilities and education abroad. The Access Abroad Web site houses, among other resources, an accommodations request form, a form that can be used to assess overseas site accessibility, a student predeparture checklist, interviews with students with disabilities who studied abroad, tips from former students, and sample accessibility summaries for specific overseas sites. (www.umabroad.umn.edu/professionals/php) (www.umabroad.umn.edu/students/identity/php)

IIE

The Institute of International Education published annual information on education abroad and international student enrollment patterns. (iie.org)

Maximizing Study Abroad

University of Minnesota faculty and staff have created guides that
address predeparture preparation, on-site learning, and reentry tips.
The guides offer a wealth of resources useful for all students that are
not written specifically for students with disabilities. (www.carla
.umn.edu/maxsa/guides.html)

Mobility International, USA

Mobility International, USA, is a nonprofit organization dedicated to
fostering international experiences for individuals with disabilities.
Its federally funded National Clearinghouse on Disability and
Exchange's comprehensive Web site offers recruitment and advising
tools and information on overseas disability preparations, resources,
and organizations. (www.miusa.org/ncde)
NAFSA: Association of International Educators is the primary professional
organization for international educators. Its publications include
resources on education abroad and assisting students with disabilities
pursuing study overseas. (www.nafsa.org/publications)

The University of Pittsburgh

The University of Pittsburgh's education abroad office received private
funding to create a DVD regarding students with disabilities and
education abroad. This DVD, available online, includes helpful
insights from overseas advisors on servicing students with disabilities.
(http://www.abroad.pitt.edu)

Reference

Institute on International Education. *Fast Facts 2010*. Retrieved April 28, 2011, from
http://www.iie.org/en/Research-and-Publications/Open-Doors).

*HEIDI M. SONESON and SHELLY FISHER are program directors in the Learning
Abroad Center at the University of Minnesota and advise students with disabilities who study abroad.*

NEW DIRECTIONS FOR STUDENT SERVICES • DOI: 10.1002/ss

7

Understanding the issues, concerns, and experience of students with psychiatric disabilities assists colleges in creating conditions of inclusion and integration in the campus environment.

Understanding the Experiences of Students with Psychiatric Disabilities: A Foundation for Creating Conditions of Support and Success

Holley A. Belch

> With all of our students, we have an obligation not only to recognize their struggles but also to identify ways in which we can help them transform struggle into accomplishment, disappointment into satisfaction, and presence into participation.
>
> Holley A. Belch (2000)

As Korbel, McGuire, Banerjee, and Saunders explain in Chapter Four (this volume), 11 percent of students in postsecondary education have a disability (National Center for Education Statistics, 2006; U.S. Government Accountability Office, 2009). Success in the K-12 system brought about by legislation (Individuals with Disabilities Education Act, 1997) and the use of individualized educational plans has made higher education possible and more attractive to students with disabilities (Wolanin and Steele, 2004). It is a reasonable assumption that as more students with disabilities in primary and secondary schools are successful in completing their education, more will enroll in postsecondary education. The increasing proportion of students with disabilities entering higher education over the past twenty-five years validates those assumptions.

One of the fastest-growing categories of disability in the college student population is psychiatric disabilities: bipolar disorder, anxiety disorders, and borderline personality disorders, among other (Eudaly, 2002;

NEW DIRECTIONS FOR STUDENT SERVICES, no. 134, Summer 2011 © Wiley Periodicals, Inc.
Published online in Wiley Online Library (wileyonlinelibrary.com) • DOI: 10.1002/ss.396

Kadison and DiGeronimo, 2004; Kampsen, 2009). The challenges in service delivery, support, policy development and implementation, retention, and successful integration into the campus community are distinct for this subpopulation. The specific skills and knowledge that student affairs practitioners and faculty need to support the success of these students are not understood universally. This subgroup of students presents new challenges to faculty and administrators who are not familiar with the needs of the population. As a result, college administrators need to examine ways to move beyond compliance with federal legislation and create environments that offer meaningful access, full integration and inclusiveness, and opportunity for educational success (Belch, 2000).

Appropriate treatment and support can provide students with psychiatric disabilities the opportunity to develop their talents and realize their potential, culminating in their successful navigation of college (Collins and Mowbray, 2005). Yet these disabilities are the least understood and least academically supported on campus (Megivern, Pellerito, and Mowbray, 2003). The fundamental challenge for student affairs professionals is that their educational and experiential preparation has not accounted for the complexity of working with students with psychiatric disabilities. Characteristically, disability support providers are the experts; however, the issues and concerns extend far beyond the work of disability support providers and must include generalist student affairs practitioners, administrators, and faculty (Kitzrow, 2003).

This chapter examines the population, describes the prevalence of this group on college campuses, offers a definition of psychiatric disability, and addresses the issues, concerns, and experiences of these students, faculty, and student affairs professionals. This chapter also addresses the value of inclusion and integration of students with psychiatric disabilities on college campuses, offers strategies for inclusion and integration in and outside the classroom, and provides a comprehensive model of support.

Population Description

Students with psychiatric disabilities are unique among the larger population of students with disabilities. Since the range of disabilities is psychiatric in nature, they are also complex and hidden, and often these students have multiple disabilities. They are the most recent subgroup of students to challenge the conventions of higher education and gain access (Nolan and others, 2005).

Definition of Psychiatric Disability

Mental illness, psychological disorder, and *psychiatric disorder* are used interchangeably to describe individuals with specific types of medical conditions. The National Institute of Mental Health 2010 provides this definition:

NEW DIRECTIONS FOR STUDENT SERVICES • DOI: 10.1002/ss

"Mental illnesses are medical conditions that disrupt a person's thinking, feeling, mood, ability to relate to others, and daily functioning." It is important to note that a mental illness does not necessarily mean that the individual has a disability covered by the protections afforded by the Americans with Disabilities Act (1990). The substantive difference between mental illness and psychiatric disability is the effect on one's capacity to cope with typical demands in life. A mental illness becomes a disability when one's ability to cope successfully is compromised. Psychiatric disability indicates that the mental illness interferes with major life activities (Souma, Rickerson, and Burgstahler, 2002). The Americans with Disabilities Act Amendments Act (ADAAA) (2008) expanded the list of major life activities to include learning-related activities such as concentrating, reading, and thinking.

Types of Psychiatric Disability Among the College Population

Psychiatric disabilities are complex and involve a wide array of disorders, including major depression and mood disorders, anxiety disorders (such as panic, obsessive compulsive, posttraumatic stress), autism spectrum disorders and Asperger's, borderline personality disorders, and psychotic and thought disorders such as schizophrenia and bipolar disorder. Each of these disorders is distinct, has unique symptoms, and is managed differently for varying students. It is important to acknowledge that one of the anxiety disorders, posttraumatic stress disorder (PTSD), can occur following any unusually traumatic event such as rape, war, natural disasters, or physical violence (Hemsley, 2010). Thus, PTSD can affect a great range of students and is not exclusive to returning war veterans, although it is prevalent in that population (Scioli, Otis, and Keane, 2010). In some cases, such as borderline personality disorder, which occurs in early adulthood and primarily in women, the difficulties rest with self-image, identity, unstable interpersonal relationships, emotional instability, self-injury, and impulsivity with substance abuse, sex, spending, reckless driving, or binge eating that is damaging (Paris, 2007). For these students, developmentally appropriate tasks such as understanding self, identity, maintaining emotional health and balance, and forming healthy interpersonal relationships may be overshadowed by the disorder.

Types of psychiatric disabilities protected by ADAAA (2008) are depression, bipolar affective disorder, borderline personality disorder, schizophrenia, anxiety disorders, obsessive-compulsive disorder, and eating disorders. Some individuals have more than one mental illness (Kiuhara and Huefner, 2008; National Institute of Mental Health, 2010), which complicates treatment and symptom management. The research and literature indicate that mental health issues are persistent and cyclical in nature and not transient (Zivin and others, 2009; Mowbray, Bybee, and Collins, 2001; Weiner and Wiener, 1996), adding to the complexity of treatment and the evaluation of support services.

Among students with psychiatric disabilities who register with campus disability services, the most common types of disorders are affective disorders, psychotic disorders, anxiety disorders, and mixed disorders (Collins and Mowbray, 2005). Perhaps as important as delineating the types of psychiatric disability is the notion that they are unique to each student, and the range of support and the differences in support are unique as well (Ekpone and Bogucki, n.d.).

Scope of Psychiatric Disability Among the College Population

Determining the prevalence of students with psychiatric disabilities in postsecondary education is not an exact science. Census data have revealed that 16 million individuals have a psychiatric disability (U.S. Census Bureau, 2006), while other sources say that approximately one in four Americans (age eighteen and older) has a mental disorder (Kessler and others, 2005; National Institute of Mental Health, 2010). The considerably high rate of prevalence in the general population has translated to increases in attendance at postsecondary institutions (Eudaly, 2002; Sharpe and others, 2004).

Substantial increases in college attendance among students with psychiatric disabilities occurred between 1978 and 1998 from an estimated 2.6 percent to 9.0 percent, respectively (Collins, 2000). More recently, estimates indicate students with psychiatric disabilities represent 15 to 20 percent of this subpopulation (Rickerson, Souma, and Burgstahler, 2004). Although an exact percentage of college students with psychiatric disabilities is unknown (Rickerson, Souma, and Burgstahler, 2004; Sharpe and others, 2004), that the numbers on college campuses are growing is undeniable (Collins and Mowbray, 2005; Eudaly, 2002; Sharpe and others, 2004). This increase is attributable to a number of factors, including an increase in the general population, criteria for diagnosis that have expanded to include a broader range of disorders (Sharpe and others, 2004; Weiner and Wiener, 1996), and student desire to attend higher education. For example, twenty years ago, college was not an option for students with Asperger's syndrome, yet more students with this disorder list attending college as their primary goal (Graetz and Spampinato, 2008). Advances in diagnosis and treatment (Eudaly, 2002; Sharpe and others, 2004, Weiner and Wiener, 1996) and improvements in medications and rehabilitation practices offer opportunities for coping successfully with life activities (Belch and Marshak, 2006; Eudaly, 2002). In addition, several psychiatric disorders become apparent between eighteen and twenty-five years of age, after the student enrolls in college (Becker and others, 2002; Collins, 2000; Sharpe and others, 2004).

The difficulty with seeking a precise determination of the number of students with psychiatric disabilities on campus is rooted in several key

NEW DIRECTIONS FOR STUDENT SERVICES • DOI: 10.1002/ss

issues. Data collected by government agencies, postsecondary institutions, and through national surveys are in a self-report format. Ostensibly the self-report nature of the information belies its reliability beyond estimates. Fear of disclosure prohibits some individuals from revealing a diagnosis, and others may be unaware of the presence of a mental illness.

Complicating matters further, identifiable categories included on these surveys were not developed universally or accepted (Wolanin and Steele, 2004). Specifically, designations of psychiatric disability differ across instruments. Significant changes in survey language have resulted in increases in the reporting of mental illness among college students. The inclusion of mental illness as a primary condition on one national survey resulted in substantial representation of these students among all students with disabilities (HEATH, 2009). Ultimately, expanded definitions of disability have contributed to the increasing numbers in the population (Hayward, 2005). Significantly, these types of surveys account for only known disabilities, not for those that students may develop while they are at college (Albrecht, 2005).

In addition, some college students are undiagnosed with a mental illness or psychiatric disorder. As noted, some disorders emerge in early adulthood, while others may be undiagnosed throughout the teen years or earlier. Undiagnosed disorders present challenges in behavioral crises to campus staff but also to the student and family, who may struggle with a diagnosis. Ultimately the extent of the undiagnosed population is unknown.

In the absence of precise statistical data, the documented rise in the number of students with mental illness, diagnosed and undiagnosed, who are seeking services at campus counseling centers supports the analogy of a "rising tide" (Eudaly, 2002, p. 1). Research and the literature have consistently affirmed the increasing treatment numbers, complexity of issues, and level of severity of mental health problems (Benton and others, 2003; Collins and Mowbray, 2005; Gallagher, 2002, 2008, 2009; Kadison and DiGeronimo, 2004; Rando, Barr, and Aros, 2008). In 2009, 25 percent of students using counseling services were on psychiatric medication, an increase from 20 percent in 2003, 17 percent in 2000, and 9 percent in 1994 (Gallagher, 2009). However, despite these reports, a relatively small number of the overall population on campus experiencing symptoms of mental illness seeks counseling (Cooper, Corrigan, and Watson, 2003). Although the Gallagher (2002, 2008, 2009) studies and others help put into perspective the changes over time in counseling service delivery and use, these data represent only students who seek mental health services.

It is clear that this subpopulation has arrived and is in need of services. How successful campus administrators are in providing appropriate support to these students and a viable knowledge base to other constituencies on campus will determine in part the level of inclusion and integration these students experience in the campus community.

Inclusion and Integration on Campus

Historically the value of access to higher education has expressed and experienced the value of educational access through legal mandates. There is a significant difference, however, between legislating access and truly creating acceptance, inclusion, and integration into a campus community. Although underrepresented groups have had different experiences, a commonality endures: some barriers exist to a fully welcoming and inclusive environment (Hall and Belch, 2000).

From the disability community perspective, inclusion refers to the concept of encouraging and welcoming individuals with disability into higher education. This idea includes the use of various formalized models of support, some involving integration into the campus community and others advancing a more segregated approach, particularly for individuals with severe disabilities. From a student affairs and higher education perspective, *inclusion* and *integration* refer to a sense of belongingness, connectedness, and full, meaningful participation in the college experience. At its base level, "inclusion implies that individuals are active members of a work and learning environment" (Kalivoda, 2009, p. 3). In order to achieve inclusion and integration for students with psychiatric disabilities, campus constituents need to anchor their thoughts, ideas, and action plans to the core values of the student affairs profession.

Core Values. The core values of human dignity, equality, and community have grounded the student affairs profession for quite some time (Belch, 2000) and are essential to creating inclusive campus environments (Hall and Belch, 2000). Societal culture dehumanizes and even demonizes individuals with mental illness. The language about mental illness reflects this, as terms such as *loony, fruitcake,* and *space cadet* are used to describe those thinking or behaving in ways that are outside the boundaries of the cultural norm. Speaking to the value of the human dignity of people with mental illness, Hall and Belch (2000) affirmed that "we need to honor individual identity, confront dehumanizing behavior, and clearly affirm the value of their involvement and what they bring to campus communities" (p. 11). In addition, Boyer (1990) espoused the importance of dignity and civility as he confirmed the need for and importance of developing community on college campuses.

The value of equality focuses on groups rather than individuals. People with psychiatric disabilities indeed represent a marginalized group both in and outside higher education. Student affairs professionals must welcome each group while developing their knowledge base and skills to provide programs, policies, and services that offer opportunities for success (Hall and Belch, 2000). It is also important to keep in mind that a group is made up of individuals, and recognizing individual differences is important, a particularly salient point about psychiatric disabilities.

New Directions for Student Services • DOI: 10.1002/ss

Community as a value is a fundamental aspect of the heritage of student affairs (Hall and Belch, 2000). The need for community and the desire to be a member is both primal and practical (Bogue, 2002), and at the center of the ideals of community is the connection to one another as human beings. Consequently community emerges when the desire to assist others reach an educational goal motivates members to engage one another, do something differently, or try something new (Roberts, 1993). In embracing the value of community, it is necessary to be mindful of the delicate balance between competing values such as rights and responsibilities, justice and mercy, diversity and community, and access and excellence (Bogue, 2002). The challenge of discovering and maintaining this balance motivates us to create opportunities for engagement with one another—the essence of community. A commitment to these values is imperative in working with students who need individualized consideration in order to meet educational goals (Hall and Belch, 2000). Commitment can take many forms, but at its core, it is the bridge connecting values with behaviors, attitudes, and language.

Social and Academic Integration. The notions of engagement and integration are vital to developing a sense of belonging, feeling connected to others, and ultimately becoming part of a community. Full integration and inclusion in a campus community can be a challenging process for any student and more so for some students with psychiatric disabilities. Tinto (1993) indicated that as students make the transition to college and try to integrate into the academic and social aspects of college life, they experience three stages: separation, transition, and incorporation.

Separation, occurring prior to and at the beginning, requires the student to detach from previous communities in order to embrace the new campus community (Tinto, 1993). For a student lacking self-advocacy skills and social skills and who is reluctant to self-disclose his or her psychiatric disability, the separation stage may be particularly difficult. The task is essentially to disconnect from the roles others have played, learn necessary new skills, and assume those new roles. For a student who needs predictability and routine for symptom management and is uncertain in new environments, this is a considerable challenge and extends well beyond the typical developmental tasks of independence and autonomy.

Transition occurs after successful completion of the separation stage yet prior to fully integrating into the campus culture. The in-between aspect of this stage, often characterized by a feeling of not belonging, can serve as a source of significant stress, which may exacerbate symptoms and potentially make it more difficult for a student to practice effective coping techniques. Group membership influences incorporation, which is vital to a sense of belonging. Social connections with peers are a significant aspect of inclusion (Hafner, 2008), yet students with differing types of psychiatric disabilities, such as borderline personality disorder or Asperger's syndrome, may find social interaction particularly challenging—and each for different reasons. With Asperger's syndrome the affected student may not understand the nuances of social communication, which often leads to behavior that may seem strange to others (Graetz and Spampinato, 2008). For example, a student with Asperger's syndrome who has been accused of stalking another student may just be romantically interested in the other person yet lack the social skills to express his feelings appropriately. As a result, others misunderstand his behavior.

The importance of inclusive environments both in and out of the classroom cannot be understated (see Chapter Three, this volume). Universal design in the classroom can also help mediate some of the functional limitations students with psychiatric disabilities experience (Souma and Casey, 2008).

Inclusive cocurricular environments are ones in which individualism is recognized and acknowledged, and membership and participation at the group level are welcomed and encouraged. Creating and facilitating inclusiveness is at the heart of student affairs work. Given that many students with psychiatric disabilities do not disclose their disability, how do student affairs staff create inclusive opportunities, environments, and conditions for them? Many of the retention principles that focus on integration into the campus community are applicable, such as promoting interaction among students, faculty, and staff (Astin, 1993). Just as important, universal design principles apply to the cocurricular environment, and Higbee and Goff (2008) offer a solid understanding and foundation for their application across functional areas. The notions of inclusion and integration naturally imply acceptance, leading to active participation in all aspects of the environment. The benefits to students with psychiatric disabilities include improved communication and social skills and access to socially appropriate role models (Alper, 2003).

Issues and Concerns. Issues, concerns, and challenges exist on campuses for all students, yet for students with psychiatric disabilities, they are particularly poignant. These barriers to success range from developmental tasks and functional limitations to social limitations, stigma, and financial concerns, and they may have an impact on students' opportunities for academic and social integration, their willingness to disclose their disability and seek support services as needed, and their ability to complete a degree. Institutional issues include a lack of information, knowledge, and training among faculty, administrators, and student affairs staff; limited human and financial resources; and the presence of institutionalized stigma and fear. The combination of student and institutional challenges serves to threaten the success of these students and perpetuate the revolving-door concept that higher education has experienced with other underrepresented groups in the past.

Barriers to Success

In referring to students with disabilities, Wolanin and Steele (2004) aptly note, "In higher education, the student is protected against discrimination and provided an equal opportunity, but there is no process aimed at achieving success" (p. viii). There is no shortage of barriers to success for college students with psychiatric disabilities. The adjustment to college, coupled with developmental issues and disability-related symptom management, functional and social limitations, attitudes and perceptions, and institutional policies and procedures are additional stressors students with psychiatric disabilities must contend with during college that affect their persistence, retention, and ability to earn a degree.

Developmental Transitions and Adjustment to College. The transition to college for many students is challenging and includes dealing with several key developmental tasks. Developmental issues for students at this stage are social and emotional: identity, autonomy, managing emotions, and developing interpersonal relationships (Chickering and Reisser, 1993). Students with psychiatric disabilities may have more difficulty or experience delays with these tasks (Ekpone and Bogucki, n.d.; Kampsen, 2009).

The energy and time that students spend in adjusting to college can be overwhelming for some, and particularly for students with psychiatric disabilities. In fact, they may need to focus their energy and efforts more on coping with the symptoms of their illness and the associated stress that accompanies it (Clark and Davis, 2000). The delay or disruption in the developmental process can then complicate the transition to college, integration into the social and academic environment, and the overall adjustment of these students (Kampsen, 2009). Thus, there is an inherent discord for these students between the timing of their developmental transitions and their adjustment to college.

Functional and Social Limitations. Among the barriers to full participation are the functional and social limitations of a mental illness. Psychiatric disorders can interfere with concentration, motivation, memory, making decisions, and social interactions (Megivern, Pellerito, and Mowbray, 2003; Weiner and Wiener, 1996). Students may experience difficulty screening out stimuli (sights, smells, sounds), coping with unexpected changes in assignments or exams, sustaining their concentration (easily distracted, difficulty following verbal instructions), managing deadlines and prioritizing, interpreting criticism or determining what to improve on, and severe test anxiety (Mancuso, 1990; Mrazek, 2002). Consequently, low self-esteem and anxiety affect their academic performance, coping skills, and class attendance (Collins and Mowbray, 2005).

Medications can produce drowsiness, causing a slow response time and affecting stamina in class (Mancuso, 1990; Mrazek, 2002). Interacting with others may prove challenging and interfere with a student's ability to fit in, get along with others, and read social cues (Mancuso, 1990; Mrazek, 2002). For some specific types of psychiatric disorders, a fear of authority exists, limiting the student's desire or ability to interact with faculty. The absence of self-advocacy skills may interfere with a student's ability to seek services (Olney and Brockelman, 2003).

The most common student concerns reported focus on accommodations and support, coping with school, and attending classes (Collins and Mowbray, 2005). Often these students are unaware of support services, have difficulty identifying services, or lack knowledge of their disability (Blacklock, Benson, and Johnson, 2003; Collins and Mowbray, 2005; Megivern, Pellerito, and Mowbray, 2003). In locating services on campus, they may be overwhelmed with the process of registering for them. Although lack of financial resources is a concern of many college students, students with psychiatric disabilities are increasingly concerned about inadequate insurance coverage, the cost of medications, and the cost of testing to confirm a diagnosis (Blacklock, Benson, and Johnson, 2003), and as a result, they often drop out (Megivern, Pellerito, and Mowbray, 2003).

Attitudes and Perceptions. Individuals with psychiatric disabilities can lead healthy and productive lives. Improvements in medications and therapies have permitted these individuals to establish and reach their personal and educational goals, yet societal discrimination and stigma threaten their treatment, success, and achievements. A hierarchy of acceptance of disability is very real, and physical and sensory disabilities are more accepted than hidden disabilities (Corrigan and Penn, 1999; Rickerson, Souma, and Burgstahler, 2004). "Perhaps the greatest barrier for persons with a psychiatric disability to achieving psychosocial adaptation is not the disability, but rather the stigma attached to it by members of society" (McReynolds and Garske, 2003, p. 14). Stigma can be as debilitating as the diagnosis of mental illness (Link and others, 2001).

Stigma is the most common reason that students with psychiatric disabilities choose not to disclose their disability (Collins and Mowbray, 2005). Discrimination and stigma lead to a sense of alienation and isolation, as well as feelings of inferiority. Students often experience a sense of social distance or avoidance by others (Link and Phelan, 1999). "This sense of alienation generated through stigma-tainted campus interactions seems to clearly place students with psychiatric disabilities at risk for leaving college" (Megivern, Pellerito, and Mowbray, 2003, p. 227).

The presence of stigma also deters students from using campus counseling and mental health services (Cooper, Corrigan, and Watson, 2003; Golberstein, Eisenberg, and Gollust, 2008). At the college level, however, disclosure is necessary for students to receive appropriate accommodations and support. Students aware of social stigma may not disclose as they enter the institution in order to free themselves of prejudice, discrimination, and a perception of limited abilities that accompany life with a psychiatric disorder (Kadison and DiGeronimo, 2004; Mrazek, 2002; Phelan and Basow, 2007).

Evidence confirms that the reluctance to disclose a psychiatric disability is well founded. Concerned about stigmatization by faculty and other students, respondents reported being embarrassed to ask for help (Collins and Mowbray, 2005; Olney and Brockelman, 2003; Sharpe and others, 2004). Students who did disclose to faculty reported an array of responses that included negative reactions, such as faculty who believed the students were faking an illness or faculty and other students who expressed resentment about the accommodations (Collins and Mowbray, 2005; Olney and Brockelman, 2003; Rickerson, Souma, and Burgstahler, 2004). Research done with faculty on this subject appears to validate the student experience. Some faculty reported a willingness to accommodate students, yet others refused to acknowledge the disability, harbored feelings of anger toward them, viewed these students as less competent, and believed they should not be on campus (Becker and others, 2002; Brockelman, Chadsey, and Loeb, 2006; Collins and Mowbray, 2005; Olney and Brockelman, 2003; Rickerson, Souma, and Burgstahler, 2004). The source of stigma from faculty is believed to be based on a lack of awareness and training (Belch and Marshak, 2006; Collins and Mowbray, 2005; Eudaly, 2002; Olney and Brockelman, 2003). Faculty awareness and knowledge are significant since students view faculty attitudes as crucial to their success (Albrecht, 2005).

Despite a rather grim picture of the impact of stigma on college students, some studies have revealed the promise of awareness and education. Individuals familiar with mental illness are less likely to support stigma and discrimination (Corrigan and Penn, 1999; Corrigan and others, 2001a, 2001b). Faculty with personal experience with psychiatric disabilities (self, friend, spouse, another student) are far more comfortable in their ability to work with students with psychiatric disabilities (Brockelman, Chadsey, and Loeb, 2006).

Persistence and Retention. A troubling issue for students with disabilities in general is their ability to persist and earn a degree. Students with psychiatric disabilities are at even greater risk. In fact, 86 percent of students with psychiatric disorders withdraw from college (Collins and Mowbray, 2005). The literature on retention and persistence is clear about the heavy toll and costs associated with retention for both the institution and the student (Braxton, Hirschy, and McClendon, 2004; Tinto, 1993).

Students with psychiatric disabilities face an assortment of barriers to success that in large part are associated with the disability itself. Social isolation, withdrawal, and academic failure are stressors that these students experience (Blacklock, Benson, and Johnson, 2003). The negative impact a psychiatric disability can have on learning, academic performance, social integration, and retention has been affirmed over time (Becker and others, 2002; Kadison and DiGeronimo, 2004; Schwartz, 2006). The cyclical nature of the illness compounds these issues (Mowbray, Bybee, and Collins, 2001; Weiner and Wiener, 1996). Essentially, managing life as a student and the disability is difficult (Blacklock, Benson, and Johnson, 2003). Moreover, the issues and concerns related to psychiatric disability extend to other members of the campus community.

Faculty and Staff Concerns and Issues

Students with psychiatric disorders have the potential to affect a broad range of the campus community, including faculty, student affairs staff, campus security, and other students as well (Kitzrow, 2003). Their presence has been a source of uneasiness among some faculty and staff, in part due to several highly visible and tragic events on campuses in recent years. In reality, there is no greater risk of violence by individuals with mental illness than by those without (Cornell, 2010; Freidl, Lang, and Scherer, 2003).

Faculty may experience anxiety or fear in dealing with this student subpopulation, which in turn has an impact on the students' academic performance (Sharkin, 2006). Faculty attitudes toward students with hidden disabilities are less positive than toward students with disabilities in general, and particularly for psychiatric disabilities (Becker and others, 2002; Keefe, 2007). In addition, some teaching styles are less effective in establishing a welcoming environment, engaging students, and promoting learning (see Chapter Three, this volume).

The most common requests for assistance from faculty and staff are for more general information and specifically classroom management and safety information (Collins and Mowbray, 2005). Other concerns focus on maintaining academic standards, receiving information on course modifications, and understanding their rights and responsibilities as well as those of the students (Salzberg and others, 2002). Faculty may simply be unfamiliar with the necessary resources or services on campus or uncomfortable approaching a student, or they may not recognize the student's need for a referral (Becker and others, 2002; Schwartz, 2006). Training has produced more positive attitudes and greater confidence in the ability of faculty to discuss concerns with students or to encourage them to seek help (Becker and others, 2002).

The lack of disclosure by students with psychiatric disabilities can be frustrating to student affairs staff because they want to help students achieve success, and they may dislike taking a reactionary posture when a student has a behavioral crisis (Belch and Marshak, 2006). However, some students have no need to disclose their psychiatric disability. In fact, some students with psychiatric disabilities have learned to manage their symptoms successfully through a variety of support mechanisms, and thus their behavior never approaches the threshold of interpretation as disruptive or problematic. Undoubtedly dealing with disruptive behavior in multiple settings such as residence halls, classrooms, the library, and campus public spaces is stressful for professional and paraprofessional staff. Despite staff concern about their lack of knowledge, they have expressed supportive attitudes and interest in learning more about the population and how to serve these students more effectively (Collins and Mowbray, 2005).

Counseling center staff and disability service providers are under increasing stress to address the volume of student mental health issues and to do so comprehensively yet with limited or diminishing resources and a heightened sensitivity to liability concerns and privacy issues (Cooper, 2006, cited in Schwartz, 2006). In turn, staff may not have sufficient training to work with this population and yet feel the pressure of others who expect them to have expertise in this area. This may be particularly acute for campuses with one or just a few staff in these areas or insufficient support services in the community, such as access to psychiatrists (Belch and Marshak, 2006).

At times viewed as a complication, privacy legislation such as the Family Educational Rights and Privacy Act of 1974 and the Health Insurance Portability and Accountability Act of 1996 can impede staff efforts as well (Belch and Marshak, 2006). The delicate balance between respecting privacy and communicating with appropriate campus entities about a student, the rights of the individual, and the rights of others in the environment pose significant challenges and subsequent dissatisfaction among campus administrators and staff (Belch and Marshak, 2006). Liability concerns extend to all parties involved. Administrators and student affairs staff are keenly aware of the consequences of wrongful-death actions and involuntary withdrawal cases levied against their institution.

At the institutional level, a lack of coordinated services, problematic communication patterns, and minimal collaborative efforts are challenging to all involved and have an adverse impact on students (Blacklock, Benson, and Johnson, 2003). A lack of connection between campus staff and community mental health professionals can significantly affect the success of these students (Megivern, 2001). Budget constraints have forced some campuses to shift philosophically from a prevention and education model to a crisis intervention and management model, exposing them to legal and ethical risks (Kadison and DiGeronimo, 2004).

There is no doubt that faculty, staff, and others on college campuses are concerned about the increase in students with psychiatric disorders. How successful campus administrators and faculty are in providing appropriate support and education will determine in part the level of inclusion and integration these students experience in the campus community.

Strategies for Success

Developing appropriate and effective campuswide strategies to support the success of students with psychiatric disabilities may appear to be a daunting task. However, higher education has consistently developed models of support for underrepresented students as each new group gained access. In working with students with psychiatric disabilities, assisting them with their transition to college and social and academic integration, and meeting their educational goals requires an awareness of both the specific disability itself and successful strategies of support. A multifaceted approach that includes educational and environmental initiatives, sources of support for

students and the campus community, and attention to policy and procedures is necessary. A comprehensive approach offers the greatest opportunity for success to the student and creates a community support model.

Educational Initiatives. A significant measure on any campus is
increasing the community's awareness of and knowledge about mental
illness (Kiuhara and Huefner, 2008). This helps to dispel myths and fears
and is critical to reducing stigma (Collins and Mowbray, 2005; Kiuhara and
Huefner, 2008). All constituencies (students, faculty, staff, campus police,
and parents and other family) need to understand the myths of mental
illness, how to identify and reach out to students in distress, and how to
refer them. Parents and guardians of students diagnosed with a psychiatric
disability can be an important source of encouragement to the student to
seek services. Faculty members need specific guidance with curricular
modifications, classroom management, and understanding resources on
campus (Eells, 2008). Furthermore, faculty and staff need to understand
basic ways to differentiate among troubling, disruptive, and threatening
behavior. Campus models of faculty training include addressing knowledge-
based issues at new faculty orientation, through campus-based teaching
excellence centers, and with resources or training modules available in
online formats.

Educational outreach to all campus constituencies needs to embrace
multiple modalities. Access to information and training resources is essential (Blacklock, Benson, and Johnson, 2003; Eells, 2008). Hard copy materials and Web site information can offer information on services and
resources. Technology can be used effectively for online self-assessment
tools, stress management materials, and training. The online environment
is particularly helpful to those who are reluctant to disclose their disability
and seek face-to-face help (Owen and Radolfa, 2009). Campus speaker
series and other public programming can address mental illness issues.
Turning to external resources such as the University of Washington's DO-IT
Web site of materials can be an especially valuable tool in providing a wide
array of resources for all constituents. Community-wide messages promoting care and concern need to be conveyed throughout campus in multiple
formats and through behavior.

Environmental Initiatives. A key issue for students with psychiatric
disabilities is experiencing the campus as a community to which they fully
belong. Campus leaders need to assess the inclusiveness of the environment
by conducting an audit. Specific to this student subpopulation, questions to
be addressed include how the campus promotes inclusiveness, a sense of
belonging, and a sense of care. The audit should identify the sources of
stigma that exist on campus, explore why stigma may exist, and determine
strategies to combat it. It should also identify the challenges in addressing
one or all of these issues. (See Chapter Two, this volume, for a comprehensive
review of initiatives that prove helpful in improving the accessibility and
inclusiveness of the physical environment).

Sources of Support. Multiple departments may exist on campus to address mental health concerns in varying ways. Counseling services, disability support services, and campus health services typically provide distinct support mechanisms to students in distress, as well as those with psychiatric disabilities. Some campuses have access to community-based mental health services based on proximity.

The success of the support provided to students is based in part on the level of communication and collaboration among individuals, departments, and agencies (Blacklock, Benson, and Johnson, 2003; Owen and Radolfa, 2009). Partnerships between and among campus groups (faculty, staff, students) can maximize both resources and the benefits to students with psychiatric disabilities.

Peer Mentors. For this subpopulation, peer mentors specifically selected and trained to work with students with psychiatric disorders can help them form trusting relationships, raise their awareness of campus resources and services, offer problem-solving help, sustain motivation and optimism, and share typical student insider information on study skills, course scheduling, and selection (Albrecht, 2005; Megivern and others, 2003). Social peer mentors can help increase the social interaction among students and serve to boost their feelings of belonging and acceptance (Hafner, 2008). This model of connecting students with and without disabilities offers students with psychiatric disabilities social role models and opportunities for social integration that can create greater awareness that can lead to understanding. As an example, psychology faculty at Keene State College in New Hampshire initiated a peer mentor program aimed at providing social support and problem-solving assistance to students with Asperger's syndrome (Welkowitz and Baker, 2005). Western New England College (n.d.) offers peer mentoring programs. Through a partnership of disability services staff and psychology department faculty, a peer mentoring support program for students on the autism spectrum and with Asperger's syndrome was designed to help with personal and psychological adjustment and the transition to college.

Student Involvement. Involvement in cocurricular programs and activities is integral to shaping a comprehensive educational experience for all students. The evidence affirms the positive contributions to a variety of educational outcomes (Astin, 1993; Pascarella and Terenzini, 2005). Recognizing aspects of a student's mental illness that affect his or her involvement and creating support mechanisms to encourage or continue that involvement is essential. For example, a student with bipolar disorder who may be cycling through a manic phase may need assistance with establishing boundaries of involvement, time management, or scheduling. For students with disorders on the autism spectrum who have a singular focus or interest area, helping them identify a student organization of interest could afford them additional opportunities for social interaction and support (Okamoto, 2007).

Nationally two groups have emerged on college campuses to offer support, education, a sense of belonging, and advocacy for mental illness. The National Alliance on Mental Illness (n.d.) has extended its community support and formed chapters on college campuses for those with mental illness. Active Minds, Inc. (2011), a nonprofit organization, uses student voices to bring attention to mental health awareness, education, and advocacy on college campuses by its presence as a recognized student organization. Both groups serve similar purposes and ultimately offer a place of belonging to students with mental illness, provide peer support, and offer friends and family avenues of understanding and support. Their presence on campus as recognized student groups creates greater awareness and educational opportunity in the community.

Student Crisis Support. A comprehensive campus plan is necessary to support students who experience a mental health crisis and others in the campus community affected by it. A crisis of this nature may not necessarily be violent or threatening, but it can be disarming or disconcerting to the student, friends, classmates, faculty, or others.

A student crisis support system has the ability to identify students in distress before a crisis occurs, assess the presence of a threat, coordinate an institutional response to a crisis, and offer support to groups of students after a crisis (Eells, 2008). Depending on the campus culture, size, and staffing patterns, there may be multiple committee structures to address distinct aspects involving a variety of entities throughout campus. Ultimately a culture of cooperation augmented by collaborative work must permeate the system.

Policy and Procedures. The need for policies and procedures is paramount for supporting students with mental health issues (Eells, 2008). At a higher institutional level, it is necessary to have a group identifying and reviewing policies and procedures that support these students (Eells, 2008). Policies regarding medical leave, involuntary and voluntary withdrawal, the student code of conduct, and parental notification are necessary (Belch and Marshak, 2006; Pavela, 1990). With regard to suicide threat, Pavela (2006) specifically urges caution using automatic and inflexible policies on involuntary withdrawal. Policies need to communicate boundaries of behavior and hold students accountable for their actions (Belch and Marshak, 2006; Pavela, 2006).

How a policy or procedure is implemented may affect the benefits to students as they manage their symptoms, lives, and academic experience. For example, flexibility in class attendance policies, leave-of-absence policies, course load levels, and tuition reimbursement policies related to withdrawal offer encouragement, support, and an opportunity to continue their education. But inconsistent application of these creates problems. As important as the policies themselves is the need to follow them (Belch and Marshak, 2006). At times, however, policy may conflict with reasonable accommodations. For example, a student dealing with medication side

NEW DIRECTIONS FOR STUDENT SERVICES • DOI: 10.1002/ss

effects needs to drink fluids continuously, yet a specific type of classroom space, such as a technology lab or lecture hall, may prohibit consuming liquids. Balancing legal obligations to providing reasonable accommodations with policies and procedures designed to account for all students and the physical environment itself is no small task. The need for competent legal counsel well versed in the higher education environment is critical (Belch and Marshak, 2006).

Conclusion

One fundamental goal of higher education is to create and sustain campus communities that are welcoming, supportive, understanding, and caring. Campuses with these qualities afford all students the opportunity to learn, explore, express themselves freely, and experience a sense of connectedness and belonging in order to reach their academic goals. Students with psychiatric disabilities need campus leaders to revisit these concepts from time to time, discuss their relevance and application, and commit to the work necessary to embrace their presence and ensure their success in higher education. This is not a task relegated solely to counseling center staff or disability services providers; rather it is a shared responsibility with faculty, student affairs staff, other students, and administrators (Kitzrow, 2003). Collective efforts must focus on creating understanding, supportive educational environments, and inclusive campus communities.

References

Active Minds, Inc. Active Mind: Changing the Conversation about Mental Health. 2011. Retrieved March 7, 2010, from http://www.activeminds.org.

ADA Amendments Act of 2008. P.L.. 110-325, 29 U.S.C.S. § 705. 2008.

Albrecht, L. S. "Students with Psychiatric Disabilities." In E. E. Getzel and P. Wehman (eds.), *Going to College: Expanding Opportunities for People with Disabilities*. Baltimore, Md.: Brookes Publishing, 2005.

Alper, S. "The Relationship Between Inclusion and Other Trends in Education." In D. Ryndak and S. Alper (eds.), *Curriculum and Instruction for Students with Significant Disabilities in Inclusive Settings*. (2nd ed.) Needham Heights, Mass.: Allyn and Bacon, 2003.

Americans with Disabilities Act of 1990. 42 U.S.C.A. § 12101 et seq. 1990.

Astin, A. *What Matters in College? Four Critical Years Revisited*. San Francisco: Jossey-Bass, 1993.

Becker, M., and others. "Students with Mental Illnesses in a University Setting: Faculty and Student Attitudes, Beliefs, Knowledge, and Experiences." *Psychiatric Rehabilitation Journal*, 2002, 25(4), 359–368.

Belch, H. A. "Editor's Notes." In H. A. Belch (ed.), *Serving Students with Disabilities*. New Directions for Student Services, no. 91. San Francisco: Jossey-Bass, 2000.

Belch, H. A., and Marshak, L. E. "Critical Incidents Involving Students with Psychiatric Disabilities: The Gap Between State of the Art and Campus Practice." *NASPA Journal*, 2006, 43(3), 464–483.

Benton, S. A., and others. "Changes in Counseling Center Client Problems Across Thirteen Years." *Professional Psychology: Research and Practice*, 2003, *34*(1), 66–72.

Blacklock, B., Benson, B., and Johnson, D. "Needs Assessment Project: Exploring Barriers and Opportunities for College Students with Psychiatric Disabilities." Unpublished manuscript, University of Minnesota, 2003.

Bogue, E. G. "An Agenda for Common Caring: The Call for Community in Higher Education. In W. M. McDonald and Associates, eds., *Creating Campus Community: In Search of Ernest Boyer's Legacy*. San Francisco: Jossey-Bass, 2002.

Boyer, E. *Campus Life: In Search of Community*. San Francisco: The Carnegie Foundation for the Advancement of Teaching, 1990.

Braxton, J. M., Hirschy, A. S., and McClendon, S. A. *Understanding and Reducing College Student Departure*. San Francisco: Jossey-Bass, 2004.

Brockelman, K. F., Chadsey, J. G., and Loeb, J. W. "Faculty Perceptions of University Students with Psychiatric Disabilities." *Psychiatric Rehabilitation Journal*, 2006, *30*(1), 23–30.

Chickering, A. W., and Reisser, L. *Education and Identity*. San Francisco: Jossey-Bass, 1993.

Clark, H. B., and Davis, M. *Transition to Adulthood: A Resource for Assisting Young People with Emotional or Behavioral Difficulties*. Baltimore, Md.: Brookes Publishing, 2000.

Collins, K. D. "Coordination of Rehabilitation Services in Higher Education for Students with Psychiatric Disabilities." *Journal of Applied Rehabilitation Counseling*, 2000, *31*(4), 36–39.

Collins, M. E., and Mowbray, C. T. "Higher Education and Psychiatric Disabilities: National Survey of Campus Disability Services." *American Journal of Orthopsychiatry*, 2005, *75*(2), 304–315.

Cooper, A. E., Corrigan, P. W., and Watson, A. C. "Mental Illness Stigma and Care Seeking." *Journal of Nervous and Mental Disease*, 2003, *191*(5), 339–341.

Cornell, D. "Threat Assessment in College Settings." *Change*, 2010, *42*(1), 8–15.

Corrigan, P. W., and Penn, D. L. "Lessons from Social Psychology on Discrediting Psychiatric Stigma." *American Psychologist*, 1999, *54*(9), 765–776.

Corrigan, P. W., and others. "Familiarity with and Social Distance from People Who Have Serious Mental Illness." *Psychiatric Services*, 2001a, *52*(7), 953–958.

Corrigan, P. W., and others. "Three Strategies for Changing Attributions About Severe Mental Illness." *Schizophrenia Bulletin*, 2001b, 27(2), 187–195.

Eells, G. *College Mental Health 2008: Key Issues for Counseling Services*. PaperClip Communications Audio Conference, 2008. Available from http://www.paper-clip.com /ME2/Default.asp.

Ekpone, P. M., and Bogucki, R. *A Postsecondary Resource Guide for Students with Psychiatric Disabilities*. Washington, D.C.: HEATH Resource Center, The George Washington University, n.d.

Eudaly, J. *A Rising Tide: Students with Psychiatric Disabilities Seek Services in Record Numbers*. Washington, D.C.: National Clearinghouse on Post-Secondary Education for Individuals with Disabilities, 2002. (ED 482 375)

Family Educational Rights and Privacy Act. 20 U.S.C. § 1232g. 1974.

Freidl, M., Lang, T., and Scherer, M. "How Psychiatric Patients Perceive the Public's Stereotype of Mental Illness." *Social Psychiatry and Psychiatric Epidemiology*, 2003, *38*(5), 269–275.

Gallagher, R. *National Survey of Counseling Center Directors*. Pittsburgh, Pa.: International Association of Counseling Services, 2002.

Gallagher, R. *National Survey of Counseling Center Directors*. 2008. Retrieved Oct. 26, 2009, from http://www.education.pitt.edu/survey/nsccd/archive/2008/monograph .pdf.

Gallagher, R. *National Survey of Counseling Center Directors*. 2009. Retrieved Apr. 13, 2010, from http://www.iacsinc.org/2009%20National%20Survey.pdf.

NEW DIRECTIONS FOR STUDENT SERVICES • DOI: 10.1002/ss

Golberstein, E., Eisenberg, D., and Gollust, S. E. "Perceived Stigma and Mental Health Care Seeking." *Psychiatric Services,* 2008, *59*(4), 392–399.

Graetz, J. E., and Spampinato, K. "Asperger's Syndrome and the Voyage Through High School: Not the Final Frontier." *Journal of College Admission,* 2008, *198,* 16–24.

Hafner, D. (2008). *Inclusion in Postsecondary Education: Phenomenological Study on Identifying and Addressing Barriers to Inclusion of Individuals with Significant Disabilities at a Four-Year Liberal Arts College.* (UMI No. 3337318). Retrieved Apr. 15, 2010, from http://proquest.umi.com/pqdweb?index=1&did=1650506521&SrchMode=1&sid=1 &Fmt=6&VInst=PROD&VType=PQD&RQT=309&VName=PQD&TS=1281214769 &clientId=63512.

Hall, L. M., and Belch, H. A. "Setting the Context: Reconsidering the Principles of Full Participation and Meaningful Access for Students with Disabilities." In H. A. Belch (ed.), *Serving Students with Disabilities.* New Directions for Student Services, no. 91. San Francisco: Jossey-Bass, 2000.

Hayward, K. A. "A Hierarchy of Disability: Attitudes of People with Disabilities Toward One Another." Unpublished doctoral dissertation, University of California, Los Angeles, 2005. Retrieved Apr. 13, 2010, from ProQuest Dissertation database. (UMI No. 3190461)

Health Insurance Portability and Accountability Act. 42 U.S.C. § 1320d et seq. 1996.

HEATH. *Postsecondary Students with Disabilities: Recent Data from the 2000 National Postsecondary Student Aid Survey.* Washington, D.C.: The George Washington University, 2009.

Hemsley, C. "Why This Trauma and Why Now? The Contribution That Psychodynamic Theory Can Make to the Understanding of Post-Traumatic Stress Disorder." *Counseling Psychology Review,* 2010, *25*(2), 13–20.

Higbee, J. L., and Goff, E. (eds.). *Pedagogy and Student Services for Institutional Transformation: Implementing Universal Design in Higher Education.* Minneapolis: University of Minnesota, 2008.

Individuals with Disabilities Education Act Amendments of 1997. 20 U.S.C. § 1400. 1997.

Kadison, R., and DiGeronimo, T. F. *College of the Overwhelmed: The Campus Mental Health Crisis and What to Do About It.* San Francisco: Jossey-Bass, 2004.

Kalivoda, K. S. "Disability Realities: Community, Culture, and Connection to College Campuses." In J. L. Higbee and A. A. Mitchell (eds.), *Making Good on the Promise: Student Affairs Professionals with Disabilities.* Lanham, Md.: University Press of America, 2009.

Kampsen, A. "Personal, Social, and Institutional Factors Influencing College Transition and Adaptation Experiences for Students with Psychiatric Disabilities." Unpublished doctoral dissertation, University of Minnesota, 2009. Retrieved Apr. 15, 2010, from ProQuest Dissertation Abstracts: http://proquest.umi.com/pqdweb?index=0&sid=1& srchmode=1&vinst=PROD&fmt=6&startpage=-1&clientid=63512&vname=PQD&R QT=309&did=1950386901&scaling=FULL&ts=1299512446&vtype=PQD&rqt=309 &TS=1299512490&clientId=63512.

Keefe, M. "A Survey of Faculty Attitudes: Post-Secondary Students with Psychiatric vs. Non-Psychiatric Disabilities." Unpublished doctoral dissertation, Memorial University of Newfoundland, 2007. Retrieved Apr. 15, 2010, from ProQuest Database: http:// proquest.umi.com/pqdweb?index=5&did=1409495901&SrchMode=1&sid=3&Fmt= 6&VInst=PROD&VType=PQD&RQT=309&VName=PQD&TS=1281215043&clien tId=63512.

Kessler, R. C., and others. "Lifetime Prevalence and Age-of-Onset Distributions of DSM-IV Disorders in the National Comorbidity Survey Replication." *Archives of General Psychiatry,* 2005, *62,* 593–602.

Kitzrow, M. A. "The Mental Health Needs of Today's College Students: Challenges and Recommendations." *NASPA Journal,* 2003, *41*(1), 167–181.

Kiuhara, S. A., and Huefner, D. S. "Students with Psychiatric Disabilities in Higher Education Settings: The Americans with Disabilities Act and Beyond." *Journal of Disability Policy Studies,* 2008, *19*(2), 103–113.

Link, B. G., and Phelan, J. C. "Labeling and Stigma." In C. S. Aneshensel and J. C. Phelan (eds.), *Handbook of the Sociology of Mental Health.* New York: Kluwer Academic/Plenum Publishers, 1999.

Link, B. G., and others. "The Consequences of Stigma for the Self-Esteem of People with Mental Illnesses." *Psychiatric Services,* 2001, *52*(12), 1621–1626.

Mancuso, L. L. "Reasonable Accommodations for Workers with Psychiatric Disabilities." *Psychosocial Rehabilitation Journal,* 1990, *14*(2), 3–19.

McReynolds, C. J., and Garske, G. G. "Psychiatric Disabilities: Challenges and Training Issues for Rehabilitation Professionals." *Journal of Rehabilitation,* 2003, *69*(4), 13–18.

Megivern, D. "Educational Functioning and College Integration of Students with Mental Illness: Examining Roles of Psychiatric Symptomatology and Mental Health Service Use." Unpublished doctoral dissertation, University of Michigan, 2001. Retrieved Jan. 17, 2008, from ProQuest database: http://proquest.umi.com/pqdweb?index=37& did=726025311&SrchMode=1&sid=5&Fmt=6&VInst=PROD&VType=PQD&RQT= 309&VName=PQD&TS=1299600690&clientId=63512. (UMI No. 3029395)

Megivern, D., Pellerito, S., and Mowbray, C. "Barriers to Higher Education for Individuals with Psychiatric Disabilities." *Psychiatric Rehabilitation Journal,* 2003, *26*(3), 217–231.

Mowbray, C. T., Bybee, D., and Collins, M. "Follow-Up Client Satisfaction in a Supported Education Program. *Psychiatric Rehabilitation Journal,* 2001, *24*, 237–247.

Mrazek, S. "Psychiatric Disabilities in Postsecondary Education." Honolulu: University of Hawaii at Manoa, National Center on Secondary Education and Transition and National Center for the Study of Postsecondary Educational Supports, 2002. Retrieved Jan. 12, 2006, from http://www.rrtc.hawaii.edu/documents/products/phase3/18.pdf.

National Alliance on Mental Illness. "What Is Mental Illness"? N.d. Retrieved Mar. 13, 2008, from http://www.nami.org/template.cfm?section=about_mental_illness.

National Center for Education Statistics. *Profile of Undergraduates in U.S. Postsecondary Education Institutions: 2003-04.* Washington, D.C.: U.S. Department of Education, 2006. Retrieved June 14, 2010, from http://nces.ed.gov/fastfacts/display.asp?id=60.

National Institute of Mental Health. *The Numbers Count: Mental Disorders in America.* Bethesda, Md.: National Institute of Mental Health, 2010. Retrieved June 14, 2010, from http://www.nimh.nih.gov/health/publications/the-numbers-count-mental-disorders-in-america/index.shtml.

Nolan, J. M., and others. "A Comprehensive Model for Addressing Severe and Persistent Mental Illness on Campuses: The New Diversity Initiative." *Journal of College Counseling,* 2005, *8*, 172–179.

Okamoto, R. "An Emerging Population in Higher Education: Students with Asperger's Syndrome." *Journal of Student Affairs,* 2007, *17*, 21–29.

Olney, M. F., and Brockelman, K. F. "Out of the Disability Closet: Strategic Use of Perception Management by Select University Students with Disabilities." *Disability and Society,* 2003, *18*(1), 35–50.

Owen, J. J., and Radolfa, E. R. "Prevention Through Connection: Creating a Campus Climate of Care. *Planning for Higher Education,* 2009, *37*(2), 26–33.

Paris, J. "The Nature of Borderline Personality Disorder: Multiple Dimensions, Multiple Symptoms, But One Category." *Journal of Personality Disorders,* 2007, *21*(5), 457–473.

Pascarella, E., and Terenzini, P. T. *How College Affects Students: A Third Decade of Research.* San Francisco: Jossey-Bass, 2005.

Pavela, G. *The Dismissal of Students with Mental Disorders: Legal Issues, Policy Consider-ations and Alternative Responses*. Washington, D.C.: National Association of College and University Attorneys, 1990. (ED 410 848)

Pavela, G. "Should Colleges Withdraw Students Who Threaten or Attempt Suicide? *Journal of American College Health*, 2006, *54*(6), 367–371.

Phelan, J. E., and Basow, S. A. "College Students' Attitudes Toward Mental Illness: An Examination of the Stigma Process." *Journal of Applied Social Psychology*, 2007, *37*(12), 2877–2902.

Rando, R., Barr, V., and Aros, C. *The Association for University and College Counseling Center 2007 Directors Annual Survey, 2008*. Retrieved Feb. 19, 2009, from http://www.aucccd.org/img/pdfs/momograph_2007.pdf.

Rehabilitation Act Amendments of 1998. 29 U.S.C. § 701. 1998.

Rickerson, N., Souma, A., and Burgstahler, S. *Psychiatric Disabilities in Postsecondary Education: Universal Design, Accommodations and Supported Education*. National Capacity Building Institute on issues of transition and postsecondary participation for individuals with hidden disabilities. Waikiki, HI, 2004. Retrieved June 11, 2009, from http://www.ncset.hawaii.edu/institutes/mar2004/papers/txt/Souma_revised.txt

Roberts, D. C. "Community: The Value of Social Synergy. In R. B. Young (ed.), *Identify-ing and Implementing the Essential Values of the Profession*. New Directions for Student Services, no. 61. San Francisco: Jossey-Bass, 1993.

Salzberg, C. L., and others. "Opinions of Disability Service Directors on Faculty Train-ing: The Need, Content, Issues, Formats, Media, and Activities." *Journal of Postsec-ondary Education and Disability*, 2002, *15*(2), 101–114.

Schwartz, A. J. "Are College Students More Disturbed Today? Stability in the Acuity and Qualitative Character of Psychopathology of College Counseling Center Clients: 1992-1993 Through 2001–2002." *Journal of American College Health*, 2006, *54*(6), 327–337.

Scioli, E. R., Otis, J. D., and Keane, T. M. "Psychological Problems Associated with Operation Enduring Freedom/Operation Iraqi Freedom Deployment." *American Jour-nal of Lifestyle Medicine*, 2010, *4*(4), 349–359.

Sharkin, B. S. *College Students in Distress: A Resource Guide for Faculty, Staff, and Campus Community*. Binghamton, N.Y.: Haworth Press, 2006.

Sharpe, M., and others. "The Emergence of Psychiatric Disabilities in Postsecondary Education." *National Center on Secondary Education and Transition Issue Brief*, 2004, *3*(1). Retrieved Feb. 11, 2009, from http://www.ncset.org/publications/printresource.asp?id=1688.

Souma, A., and Casey, D. "The Benefits of Universal Design for Students with Psychiatric Disabilities." In S. E. Burgstahler and R. C. Cory (eds.), *Universal Design in Higher Edu-cation: From Principles to Practice*. Cambridge, Mass.: Harvard Education Press, 2008.

Souma, A., Rickerson, N., and Burgstahler, S. *Academic Accommodations for Students with Psychiatric Disabilities*. Seattle: DO-IT, University of Washington, 2002 Retrieved Nov. 13, 2009, from http://eric.ed.gov/ERICDocs/data/ericdocs2sql/content_storage_01/0000019b/80/1b/0e/93.pdf. http://www.eric.ed.gov.proxy.lib.wayne.edu/PDFS/ED476555.pdf

Tinto, V. *Leaving College: Rethinking the Causes and Cures of Student Departure*. (2nd ed.) Chicago: University of Chicago Press, 1993.

U.S. Census Bureau. *American Community Survey (2006)*. 2006. Retrieved May 13, 2010, from http://www.census.gov/hhes/www/disability/2006acs.html.

U.S. Government Accountability Office. *Higher Education and Disability: Education Needs a Coordinated Approach to Improve Assistance to Schools in Supporting Students*. Washington, D.C.: U.S. Government Accountability Office, 2009.

Weiner, E., and Wiener, J. "Concerns and Needs of University Students with Psychiatric Disabilities. *Journal of Postsecondary Education and Disability*, 1996, *12*(1), 2–8.

Welkowitz, L. A., and Baker, L. J. "Supporting College Students with Asperger's Syndrome." In L. J. Baker and L. A. Welkowitz (eds.), *Asperger's Syndrome: Intervening in Schools, Clinics and Communities.* Mahwah, N.J.: Erlbaum, 2005.

Western New England College. "Peer Mentoring Support." N.d. Retrieved June 3, 2010, from http://www1.wnec.edu/academicaffairs/index.cfm?selection=doc.6686.

Wolanin, T. R., and Steele, P. E. *Higher Education Opportunities for Students with Disabilities: A Primer for Policymakers.* Washington, D.C.: Institute for Higher Education Policy, 2004.

Zivin, K., and others. "Persistence of Mental Health Problems and Needs in a College Student Population." *Journal of Affective Disorders,* 2009, *117,* 180–185.

HOLLEY A. BELCH is a professor in the Student Affairs in Higher Education Department at Indiana University of Pennsylvania.

NEW DIRECTIONS FOR STUDENT SERVICES • DOI: 10.1002/ss

8

The Americans with Disabilities Act Amendments Act (ADAAA) and new regulations by the U.S. Justice Department significantly broaden legal protections for students with disabilities. This, coupled with emerging populations with disabilities, will challenge postsecondary education to think differently about what is fundamental about their programs and the need to embrace flexibility in providing educational services.

Legal Issues in Serving Students with Disabilities in Postsecondary Education

Jo Anne Simon

For decades, postsecondary institutions have focused more on the line between compliance and noncompliance, balancing the rights and responsibilities of institutions with those of students with disabilities. The danger for postsecondary institutions in focusing on a "line in the sand" approach was to further perceptions that students with disabilities were getting something others were not (accommodations), thus setting up unnecessary tensions. A new era is dawning, however, led by amendments to the Americans with Disabilities Act (ADA) itself, revised regulations, the influence of technology, and new populations on campus (those with autism spectrum disorders and U.S. military veterans) that will make faculty, staff, and administrators stretch beyond their traditional comfort zones in pursuit of equal access to postsecondary education.

This chapter highlights key features in the upcoming dialogue and touches on issues that will be coming to the fore by discussing statutory and regulatory amendments, court cases, and letters of finding issued by the U.S. Department of Education's Office of Civil Rights (OCR). Since the ADA and section 504 are substantially the same as they apply to higher education, this chapter generally refers to either the ADA or section 504 of the Rehabilitation Action of 1973 (section 504).

General Obligations of Federal Disability Rights Statutes

Under section 504 and the ADA, an institution's fundamental obligation is to avoid or cease acting in a discriminatory manner. Specifically, the ADA prohibits actions that:

NEW DIRECTIONS FOR STUDENT SERVICES, no. 134, Summer 2011 © Wiley Periodicals, Inc.
Published online in Wiley Online Library (wileyonlinelibrary.com) • DOI: 10.1002/ss.397

- Deny qualified students with disabilities an equal opportunity to participate in programs or activities
- Provide aids and services that are not "equal to" or as "effective as" those provided to others
- Provide different or separate aids, services, or benefits than those necessary for providing meaningful access
- Provide significant assistance to third parties that discriminate against qualified individuals with disabilities
- Use methods of administration that result in discrimination
- Use eligibility criteria that screen out or tend to screen out individuals with disabilities
- Fail to provide reasonable accommodations

Regardless of intent, actions or inactions that have the effect of discriminating against persons with disabilities are forbidden (*Pushkin* v. *Regents of the University of Colorado*, 1981).

These obligations extend to all services, benefits, programs, opportunities, and activities to eradicate disability discrimination "stemming . . . from simple prejudice" (*Arline v. School Board of Nassau County,* 1987) and to provide reasonable accommodations. Policies, practices, and procedures may not exclude, deny opportunities to otherwise qualified students, or treat students with disabilities differently. According to the U.S. Supreme Court, institutions must not only avoid discriminating against students with disabilities, they must also make "reasonable accommodation" to best ensure "meaningful access" (*Alexander* v. *Choate* 1985, p. 301).

Postsecondary institutions must have several processes in place. First, they should have an established process for determining if accommodations should be provided to a student, and if so, what they will be. Second, their procedures must ensure that accommodations are actually provided (*Cleveland Chiropractic College,* 1995). Third, they must develop an internal grievance policy for students with disabilities that conforms to traditional notions of due process: notice, an opportunity to be heard, and an impartial finder of fact.

Who is protected is a hotly contested issue. The statutory definition of who is protected remains an individual who has a physical or mental impairment that substantially limits a major life activity, has a record of having such an impairment, or is regarded as having such an impairment. Major life activities are "those basic activities that the average person . . . can perform with little or no difficulty". 29.C.F.R. Part 1630.

In 2008, Congress dramatically altered how the language in the ADA was to be interpreted, restoring it to Congress's original intent. The ADA Amendments Act of 2008 (P.L. 110-325) clarified what it meant by terms that many courts had misconstrued. Revised regulations providing significantly broader protections were recently issued.

Congress significantly modified the law to reject four landscape-changing U.S. Supreme Court decisions (*Sutton* v. *United Airlines,* 1999;

NEW DIRECTIONS FOR STUDENT SERVICES • DOI: 10.1002/ss

Murphy v. *United Parcel Service*, 1999; *Albertson's* v. *Kirkingburg*, 1999; *Toyota Motor Manufacturing* v. *Williams*, 2002) because these cases improperly "narrowed the broad scope of protection intended to be afforded by the ADA, thus eliminating protection for many individuals whom Congress intended to protect" (42 U.S.C. § 12101(a)(4)). According to Congress, the courts had too often found that individuals needed to demonstrate a greater degree of limitation than was originally intended by Congress (42 U.S.C. § 12101(a)(7))). Congress also found that the federal regulations that had defined the term *substantially limits* as "significantly restricted" communicated a much higher standard of impairment than Congress had intended. Congress therefore changed the ADA in several important ways:

- It eliminated the U.S. Supreme Court's requirement that the ameliorative effects of "mitigating measures," such as medication, prosthetic devices, or learned compensatory methods, must be considered in assessing whether one has a disability (except for ordinary eyeglasses or contact lenses).
- It specifically provided rules of construction requiring that the ADAAA be construed in favor of broad coverage of individuals, rejecting the Supreme Court case holding that proving disability subjected ADA plaintiffs to a "strict and demanding standard" (*Toyota*, 2002).
- It expanded the illustrative list of major life activities to include sitting and standing, lifting, thinking, reading, concentrating, communicating with others, sleeping, and "major bodily functions." Because the list is not exhaustive, court decisions that found activities such as engaging in sexual relations (*McAlindin v. County of San Diego*, 1999) and test taking (*Bartlett v. New York State Board of Law Examiners*, 1998) to be major life activities remain good law.

Congress also made clear that the amendments:

- Were to shift attention from whether the individual's impairment qualified as a disability to whether discrimination had occurred
- Confirmed that individuals with episodic conditions such as recurrent depression or multiple sclerosis were protected
- Do not require a student to be severely impaired in order to be protected
- Rejected the assumption that an academically high-performing student cannot be substantially limited in activities such as learning or reading
- Confirmed that it supported the holding in *Bartlett* (1998) and stated that students with learning disabilities would be considered disabled under the law even if they managed their own adaptive strategies or received informal or undocumented accommodations that lessened

NEW DIRECTIONS FOR STUDENT SERVICES • DOI: 10.1002/ss

the deleterious effects of their disability (*Federal Register,* 2008, p. H8291)

Thus, Congress made it clear that students may be talented and gifted *and* disabled and entitled to reasonable accommodations under the ADAAA and section 504. As one member of Congress stated, "People with dyslexia are diagnosed based on an unexpected difficulty in reading. This requires a careful analysis of the method and manner in which this impairment substantially limits an individual's ability to read, which may mean taking more time—but may not result in a less capable reader" (*Federal Register 2008*, p. H8296). Although there are few cases interpreting the ADAAA yet, the federal courts have begun to take notice (*Jenkins v. National Board of Medical Examiners,* 2009). Recently the U.S. Department of Justice reached a settlement with the National Board of Medical Examiners in connection with this very issue (*National Board of Medical Examiners, 2011*).

In addition, Congress mandated that the Equal Employment Opportunity Commission revise its regulations to eliminate the offending language that had so led the courts astray. Final regulations published on March 25, 2011, take effect May 24, 2011 (*Federal Register, 2011*). Among the issues addressed and clarified in the regulations are these:

- In an analysis of whether an individual is substantially limited, the comparison to "most people" should not be mathematical and should be based on a commonsense analysis, and are to be interpreted to require a lesser degree of functional limitation than had been applied previously. When comparing individuals with impairments to "most people" the comparison will usually not require scientific, medical, or statistical analysis and that it may be helpful to consider the condition, manner, and/or duration in which a person performs an activity as compared to most people, giving consideration to "the difficulty, effort, or time required . . .; pain experienced . . .; the length of time a major life activity can be performed; and/or the way an impairment affects the operation of a major bodily function" (Federal Register, 2011).
- A physical or mental impairment is not a disability if it is both transitory and minor, but may be disabling if transitory, but substantially limiting.

Specific Applications to Postsecondary Educational Access

Access has many faces, including physical and communications access, programmatic access, and access to accommodations. The goal of access is to facilitate the increased integration of students with disabilities. Both physical and communications access, as well as program access, remain key aspects to compliance with ADA and section 504 in postsecondary education.

NEW DIRECTIONS FOR STUDENT SERVICES • DOI: 10.1002/ss

Physical Access: On and Off Campus. Students with disabilities must be given access to buildings and facilities on campus and off campus that are being used in connection with the college's courses or extracurricular activities. Moreover, both the postsecondary institution and the building being leased have obligations under the ADA. Neither can evade its obligations by assuming the other will comply.

Program Access. The term *program access* derives from section 504's provision that no person with a disability should be "subjected to discrimination under any program or activity" (29 U.S.C. § 794). Institutions are permitted to provide access to programs and activities without requiring extensive renovation or removal of architectural barriers. According to the regulations implementing section 504, the term *program* includes housing, club activities, field trips, food service, counseling, transportation, and athletics, for example.

Key Accommodation Provisions. A postsecondary educational institution must make reasonable accommodations in order to provide equal opportunity for participation in courses, programs, and activities (*Wichita State University,* 1991). Students must provide adequate notice of disability. Once the institution is notified or has "sufficient knowledge" of a student's disability, it has an obligation to reasonably accommodate (*Concepcion* v. *Puerto Rico,* 2010). The laws protect only students with disabilities who are "qualified" or able to meet the technical and academic qualifications for entry into the school or program (34 C.F.R. § 104.3(k) (3)). An institution need not provide accommodations, however, that would "fundamentally alter" the educational program or academic requirements that are essential to a program of study (*Wynne* v. *Tufts University School of Medicine,* 1991; *Wong* v. *Regents of the University of California,* 1999; (28 C.F.R § 36.303(a)). An institution is not responsible for providing personal services such as attendants, hearing aids, and glasses (28 C.F.R. § 35.135). Under the applicable regulations, tutoring has been interpreted as a personal service. Therefore, it need not be provided as an auxiliary aid or service unless it is provided to other students (*California State University, Sacramento,* 1996).

Auxiliary Aids and Services. An institution must provide auxiliary aids and services such as qualified sign language interpreters, video relay interpreting (including real-time captioning, voice, text, and video-based telecommunications products and systems), note takers, qualified readers, Braille and large-print materials, screen reader software, magnification software, optical readers, secondary auditory programs, and adaptive equipment and software. Public institutions must give "primary consideration" to the requests of persons with disabilities unless it demonstrates another existing equally effective means of communication.

Academic Adjustments. An institution must make academic adjustments to ensure that students have equal opportunities to participate in programs and activities. Academic adjustments may include extended time for tests, completion of course work, or graduation; tape recording of classes; course substitution to meet degree requirements; and modification evaluation so as not to discriminate except where such skills are specifically being measured.

Students may be expected to take on some responsibility for securing accommodations, such as asking a professor to identify a fellow student to take notes. However, if this effort did not prove successful, the institution must ensure that note-taking services are provided by other means. Students are not to be left adrift because the system did not work in a particular situation. By the same token, the student is responsible for reporting back if the established procedure did not work (*Solano Community College*, 1995).

Students may have difficulty articulating to faculty why they need the modification they are requesting and how it relates to their disability. That institutions should orient faculty to their legal obligations and assist faculty is becoming more and more important as the population of students with disabilities increasingly includes returning veterans and students with Asperger's syndrome or other autism spectrum disorders.

The Role of Technology. Colleges must ensure meaningful access to technology. Technology can open worlds of material for students with disabilities, but it can create barriers and exclude. (For a discussion of online course accessibility, see Chapter Five, this volume.) For example, purchasing technology creates an expectation that it will be accessible and suggests that the institution has the resources and expertise to fully consider the role of technology with regard to other aspects of its program (*University of California, Los Angeles*, 1997). This is consistent with reports by congressional committees at the time of the ADA's passage in 1990: "The Committee intends that the types of accommodations and services provided to individuals with disabilities, under all of the titles of this bill, should keep pace with the rapidly changing technology of the times" (House Education Committee Report, H.R. Rep. 101-485(II), 1990, p. 108).

Current Issues

New legislation and revised federal regulations have ushered in new requirements for disability services providers to balance. Standards for documenting disability have been clarified. Access to print and alternative text is required. In addition, the enrollment of military veterans in college poses new demands on service provision.

Documenting Disability. Unexpectedly the ADA resulted in a new hurdle for students with disabilities: demonstrating that they have disabilities and are entitled to protection. Extensive documentation requirements became more prevalent and pronounced after the Supreme Court's decisions in the *Sutton* trilogy of cases and in *Toyota* (2002). This has been particularly true for the so-called hidden disabilities, including learning disabilities, attention deficit hyperactivity disorder, and psychological disabilities (*Price v. National Board of Medical Examiners,* 1997; *Gonzales v. National Board of Medical Examiners,* 2000; *Wong v. Regents of University of California,* 2004).

The ADAAA makes clear that determining whether one is protected should not require "extensive analysis." Documentation requirements holding individuals to a "strict and demanding standard" that the U.S. Supreme Court articulated in *Toyota* (2002) are not in keeping with the established law, and institutions that have taken this approach are well advised to change their policies. The Association on Higher Education and Disability provides a best practices approach to documentation guidance on its Web site.

The U.S. Department of Justice (DOJ) recently amended its regulations requiring that "examinations and courses related to applications, licensing, . . . or postsecondary education, professional or trade purposes" (42 U.S.C. § 12189 (Sept 15, 2010)) must be made accessible to persons with disabilities. In doing so (even prior to ADAAA passage), the DOJ had "addressed concerns that requests by testing entities for documentation regarding the existence of an individual's disability and need for [accommodations] . . . were often inappropriate and burdensome" (Guidance on Revisions to ADA Regulation on Nondiscrimination on the Basis of Disability by Public Accommodations and Commercial Facilities, Appendix A to 28 CFR part 36 (*Federal Register,* 2010)).

Concerned by persistent reports that standardized testing entities were requiring burdensome volumes of information and extensive details about an individual's disability, questioning the documentation submitted by qualified professionals, and responding in an untimely manner to requests for accommodation, DOJ revised its regulations, commenting that

> applicants who submit appropriate documentation, *e.g.,* documentation that is based on the careful individual consideration of the candidate by a professional with expertise relating to the disability in question, should not be subjected to unreasonably burdensome requests for additional documentation. While some testing commenters objected to this standard, it reflects the Department's longstanding position (*Federal Register,* 2010).

Specifically, the regulations (which took effect on March 15, 2011) provide that

(iv) Any request for documentation, if such documentation is required, is reasonable and limited to the need for the modification, accommodation, or auxiliary aid or service requested.

(v) When considering requests for modifications, accommodations, or auxiliary aids or services, *the entity gives considerable weight to documentation* of past modifications, accommodations, or auxiliary aids or services received in similar testing situations, as well as such modifications, accommodations, or related aids and services provided in response to an Individualized Education Program (IEP) provided under the Individuals with Disabilities Education Act or a plan describing services provided pursuant to section 504 of the Rehabilitation Act of 1973, as amended (often referred to as a Section 504 Plan).

(vi) The entity responds in a timely manner to requests for modifications, accommodations, or aids to ensure equal opportunity for individuals with disabilities (28 C.F.R. § 36.309, emphasis added).

Postsecondary institutions have been relying on cases under section 309 for guidance in formulating their own documentation policies. Thus, these newly revised regulations will be critically important in the coming years, especially the DOJ's clear requirement that the opinions and recommendations of the professionals who have personally evaluated the student must be given "considerable weight" by the institution:

> When testing entities receive documentation provided by a qualified professional who has made an individualized assessment of an applicant that supports the need for the . . . accommodation . . . they shall generally accept such documentation and provide the accommodation. . . . Reports from experts [with] personal familiarity with the candidate should take precedence over those from . . . reviewers for testing agencies (*Federal Register, 2010*, p. 56297).

> In sum, an institution may not establish unduly burdensome documentation criteria or establish criteria that are inconsistent with accepted practice, especially where accepted practice requires clinical judgment. In *Bartlett* (1998), the Second Circuit found that the New York State Board of Law Examiners was not due any deference in determining whether an individual had a disability, despite the fact that it had engaged a consultant for this purpose, noting that "even where an agency has expertise, courts should not allow agency factual determinations to go unchallenged" (p. 327). This is consistent with DOJ's strengthened regulatory guidance.

The issue of what documentation is needed is likely to continue to be an issue, as are some institutions' requirements that specific type of tests or evaluations be conducted (*Bartlett*, 1998). According to DOJ, "An applicant's failure to provide results from a specific test or evaluation instrument should not of itself preclude approval of requests for . . . accommodations" (Federal Register, 2008, p. 56297) (*Bartlett*, 1998, p. 327).

Another area that continues to be the subject of discussion is the recency of documentation. The university's determination that students with learning disabilities must be reassessed every three years in order to qualify for services was the precipitating event in *Guckenberger* v. *Trustees of Boston University* (1997). The court found that since there was no science supporting this requirement, it was overly burdensome and discriminatory. DOJ's revised guidance is consistent with *Guckenberger*: "If an applicant has been granted accommodations post-high school . . . there is no need for reassessment for a subsequent examination" (*Federal Register, 2010*, p. 56297).

Access to Print or Alternate Text. Generally course materials must be made available in alternate media at the start of the semester or, at the very minimum, the time of the relevant reading assignment. Handouts must be accessible when distributed to other students. Methods of note taking must be flexible, and institutions responsible for providing certain equipment-related accommodations such as computers and tape recorders (*California Community Colleges*, 1996). An institution's policies and procedures may not result in a refusal or undue delay in service provision due to administrative convenience or otherwise (*Magill v. Board of Trustees of Iona College*, 1998).

Technology has grown by leaps and bounds since OCR first ruled on this topic. Little of what exists today was envisioned when the ADA and section 504 regulations were first promulgated. In 2009-2010, the DOJ entered into five letters of resolution with as many colleges (Reed College, Case Western Reserve, Pace University, Arizona State University, and Princeton University) for use of the Amazon Kindle DX product in pilot testing on their campuses. A Letter of Resolution is issued after the Department of Justice engages in an early dispute resolution process with an entity against whom a complaint has been lodged. Letters of Resolution provide guidance to other similarly situated entities regarding compliance. Under the above Letters of Resolution, because the Kindle controls are not currently accessible to blind students, colleges may not require its use for course study.

Colleges are expected to keep up with technological advances. So, for example, in the recent case of *Enyart v. National Conference of Bar Examiners* (NCBE) (2011), a legally blind woman with a progressive vision disorder applied to take the Multistate Professional Responsibility Exam and the Multistate Bar Exam, both of which are required to be licensed to practice law. She was denied the use of the combination of adaptive software that she normally used to read. The NCBE refused to allow her to use a combination of print enlargement and screen reader software, asserting that a reader and a closed circuit TV magnifier were sufficient, even after the plaintiff indicated that a TV magnifier made her nauseous. Enyart argued that the NCBE was obligated to "assure that . . . the examination is selected and administered so as to *best ensure* that, when the examination is administered to an individual with a disability . . . the examination results accurately reflect the individual's aptitude or achievement level" (28 C.F.R. § 36.309(b)(1)(i)). The NCBE argued it was obligated only to make the test "available" to her, that the "best ensure" language of the regulation overstepped Congress's mandate, and that she had used different accommodations on the SAT and LSAT. The Ninth Circuit Court of Appeals disagreed and held that "assistive technology is not frozen in time: as technology advances, testing accommodations should advance as well" (*Enyart*, 2011, p. 8). The court held that the issue was "not what might or might not accommodate other people with vision impairments, but what is necessary to make the[se tests]accessible to Enyart given her specific impairment and the specific nature of these exams" (p. 8).

Although courts traditionally give a great deal of deference to academic institutions' pedagogical decisions, that deference that includes the determinations of what is a reasonable accommodation is not absolute, as the U.S. Court of Appeals for the Ninth Circuit held in 1999. In *Wong* (1999), the court noted:

> Courts still hold the final responsibility for enforcing the Acts, including determining whether an individual is qualified, with or without accommodation, for the program in question. We must ensure that educational institutions are not "disguis[ing] truly discriminatory requirements" as academic decisions; to this end, "the educational institution has a 'real obligation . . . to seek suitable means of reasonably accommodating a handicapped person and to submit a factual record indicating that it conscientiously carried out this statutory obligation'" [p. 7].

College Military Veterans. An estimated 2 million American men and women will have served in the military in Iraq and Afghanistan and will be eligible for educational benefits under the Post-9/11 Veterans Assistance Act of 2008 (New G.I. Bill). A good many veterans, some estimate as many as 40 percent of Iraq and Afghanistan veterans, will come home with one or more disabling conditions (Grossman, 2009). As noted authority on postsecondary disability law Paul Grossman writes, the confluence of returning veterans, the passage of the New G.I. Bill, and the ADAAA could create a "perfect storm" on American campuses (p. 4).The integration of post-9/11 veterans on American campuses will undoubtedly challenge the way postsecondary educational institutions meet their legal and moral obligations to these individuals, the vast majority of whom come with posttraumatic stress disorder and traumatic brain injury, along with loss of limbs, disfigurement, and debilitating toxic exposure. The nature of the brain injuries caused by improvised incendiary devices, which shake the brain within the cranium even as it is protected by a combat helmet, are unfamiliar to most disability service providers, let alone most faculty and staff, but they will surely test our notions of substantial limitation. Among the other issues raised by the presence of these veterans will be the following, which will present a number of challenges:

- The way institutions think about what is fundamental to their degree programs, so as to permit the use of auxiliary aids many institutions heretofore prohibited (such as calculators in basic math courses)

- The insistence on requiring course work primarily because it has always been done that way
- Institutional inflexibility in the delivery of academic adjustments and auxiliary aids and services
- Required course and credit loads, late drops of courses, and early registration policies
- Rigidity of policies regarding documentation and accommodations
- The combinations of accommodations institutions have routinely balked at providing, for example, extended time plus off-the-clock breaks

Veterans are far less likely than other students to come to postsecondary education equipped to properly demonstrate disability or access services. Many may be in significant denial about the nature and extent of their impairments, preferring not to see themselves as disabled, but to view themselves as "wounded warriors," and they may view the use of accommodations as weakness or unfairness. Others are still learning how their disability affects them physically, socially, and emotionally.

Scholars studying this topic advise that veterans need a place on campus to be with other veterans because they have shared experiences. Creative approaches and sensitivity will be necessary to serve these students.

Other Federal Protections

The Individuals with Disabilities Education Act does not apply at the postsecondary level. The Supreme Court's requirement to have disability services professionals focus on whether a student had a disability led to a great deal of confusion as to whether evidence of special educational services was sufficient to demonstrate eligibility for the ADA's protections. With the advent of the ADAAA (which addresses the definition of disability) and the revised DOJ regulations (which address documentation), the conversation has been clarified. Service providers should no longer question the validity of Individualized Education Programs (IEPs) as some evidence of disability. However, students with disabilities may have protection in other federal statutory schemes, most notably the Family Rights and Privacy Act (FERPA), known as the Buckley amendment.

FERPA is the primary federal statute affecting disclosure of educational records, which may include disability-related information. It gives students access to their educational records and prohibits unauthorized disclosure to persons without a legitimate educational interest. It does not provide access to treatment records to the student or those with a legitimate educational interest. Conversations with students with disabilities and observations by faculty and staff are not within the reach of FERPA, but may be governed by the ADA, section 504, or state confidentiality laws, as well as state laws regarding privileged communications, such as those between doctors and patients.

Conclusion

Postsecondary institutions should review their decisions, policies, practices and procedures for compliance purposes with an open mind and an introspective analysis of the parties' preconceived notions about disability and higher education. A dose of common sense and a case-by-case review goes a long way toward ensuring compliance with the laws and the meaningful participation of students with disabilities in higher education. A truly interactive process will bring about a proper balance between the rights and responsibilities of all relevant parties. As the U.S. Supreme Court has repeatedly held, there are no absolutes in this endeavor.

References

ADA Amendments Act of 2008 (P.L. 110-325), 42 U.S.C. § 12101–12102.
Albertsons, Inc. v. Kirkingburg, 527 U.S. 555, 119 S. Ct. 2162 (1999).
Alexander v. Choate, 469 U.S. 287 (1985).
Arline v. School Board of Nassau County, 480 U.S. 273, 107 S. Ct. 1123 (1987).
Bartlett v. New York State Board of Law Examiners, 156 F.3d 321 (2d Cir. 1998), vacated and remanded, 119 S. Ct. 2388 (1999), aff'd in part & remanded, 226 F.3d 69 (2d Cir. 2000); 2001 WL 930792 (S.D.N.Y. Aug. 15, 2001).
California Community Colleges, OCR correspondence, Sept. 18, 1996.
California State University, Sacramento, OCR Case No. 09-95-2196 (Region IX, 1996).
Cleveland Chiropractic College, OCR Case No. 07-95-2051 (Region VII, 1995).
Concepcion v. Puerto Rico, 682 F. Supp. 2d 164 (D.P.R. 2010).
Enyart v. National Conference of Bar Examiners, 2011 WL9735 (9th Cir. 2011).
Family Education Rights and Privacy Act, 20 U.S.C. § 1232g.
Federal Register, September 17, 2008.
Federal Register, September 15, 2010.
Federal Register, March 25, 2011.
Gonzales v. National Board of Medical Examiners, 225 F.3d 620 (6th Cir. 2000).
Grossman, P. D. "Forward with a Challenge: Leading Our Campuses Away from the Perfect Storm." Journal of Postsecondary Education and Disability, 2009, 22(2), 4–9.
Guckenberger v. Trustees of Boston University, 974 F. Supp. 106 (D. Mass. 1997).
Individuals with Disabilities Education Act, 20 U.S.C. § 1400, et seq.
Jenkins v. National Board of Medical Examiners, 2009 US Lexis App. 2660 (6th Cir. Feb. 11, 2009).
Magill v. Board of Trustees of Iona College, 94 Civ. 9182 (S.D.N.Y. 1998).
McAlindin v. County of San Diego, 192 F.3d 1226 (9th Cir. 1999).
Murphy v. United Parcel Service, Inc., 527 U.S. 516, 119 S. Ct. 2133 (1999).
National Board of Medical Examiners (settlement with US Dep't of Justice), http://www.ada.gov/nbme.htm (Feb. 22, 2011) (last visited Mar. 12, 2011).
Price v. National Board of Medical Examiners, 966 F. Supp. 419 (S.D. W.Va. 1997).
Pushkin v. Regents of the University of Colorado, 628 F.2d 1372 (10th Cir. 1981).
Report of the Committee on Education, U.S. House of Representatives, H.R. REP. 101-485(II), H.R. REP. 101-485, 101st Cong., 2nd Sess. 1990, 1990 U.S.C.C.A.N. 303, 1990 WL 125563 (Leg.Hist.).
Solano Community College, OCR Case No. 09-94-2064-I (Region IX, 1995).
Sutton v. United Airlines, Inc., 527 U.S. 471, 119 S. Ct. 1752 (1999).
Toyota Motor Manufacturing v. Williams, 534 U.S. 184, 122 S. Ct. 681 (2002).
University of California, Los Angeles, OCR Case No. 09-97-2002 (Region IX, 1997).

Wichita State University, 2 NDLR 154 (OCR Region VII, 1991).
Wong v. Regents of the University of California, 1999 WL 717729 (9th Cir. 1999).
Wong v. Regents of University of California, 379 F.3d 1097 (9th Cir. 2004).
Wynne v. Tufts University School of Medicine, 932 F.2d 19 (1st Cir 1991)(en banc).

JO ANNE SIMON practices disability rights law in New York and is an associate professor of law at Fordham University School of Law.

NEW DIRECTIONS FOR STUDENT SERVICES • DOI: 10.1002/ss

INDEX

CPSIA information can be obtained at www.ICGtesting.com
Printed in the USA
LVOW08s0156170914

404362LV00012B/117/P